AGS

Preparing for Writing Tests

Student Activity Book

GRADES 9–12

AGS®

AGS® American Guidance Service, Inc.
4201 Woodland Road
Circle Pines, MN 55014-1796
1-800-328-2560

Printed in the United States of America

ISBN 0-7854-2475-X

Product Number: 71522

A 0 9 8 7 6 5 4 3 2 1

Contents

Contents

INTRODUCTION
About Writing Tests

What Kinds of Questions Are Asked on Tests?

Standardized tests have a number of different kinds of questions. These question types include the following:

- **Multiple Choice** These questions are common on standardized tests. They ask you to pick out the best answer from a group of choices. Multiple-choice items often appear on tests of reading, mathematics, science, and social studies skills.

- **Short Answer or Short Response** These questions ask you to write several sentences to answer a question, usually about something you have just read.

- **Essay Prompts or Extended Response** These questions appear on writing tests. A prompt asks you to write a long, organized answer called an **essay**. For that reason, writing tests are sometimes called essay tests.

This book will focus on writing tests.

What Is the Purpose of a Writing Test?

We can start to answer this question by saying what the purpose of a writing test is **not**.

- A writing test does not test you on facts you have learned in class. The prompt will give you most of the information you need. Any other information you use in your essay will come from your own experiences.

- A writing test does not measure how neatly you write. The most important thing is that you have strong, well-organized ideas. However, if your handwriting is so unclear that people cannot read it, no one will understand your ideas.

- A writing test does not measure how well you agree with your teacher (or anyone else). Many writing prompts ask you to take a side on an issue. In those cases, there is no "right" side to choose.

The purpose of a writing test is to measure how well you can join ideas and how clearly you can present them. In a writing test, you will have a limited amount of time to write your essay. Also, you will not be allowed to look in a dictionary or any other reference book. You will not even be able to ask a friend to glance at what you have written. A writing test measures your basic skill as a writer, without the aid of books, tutors, or other help.

How Are Writing Tests Graded?

Essays written for standardized tests are evaluated by professional graders, sometimes called **readers.** Test readers are carefully trained to be fair and consistent. When they are grading, they typically use a rubric. A **rubric** is a checklist containing the key elements a reader will look for in your essay. There are many different kinds of rubrics. However, most rubrics focus on the same things.

Rubrics will often direct readers to look for the following elements in an essay:

● a clear central idea, or **focus**

● points that back up the central idea

● good organization

● a definite beginning and end

● a complete answer to the prompt

● correct use of grammar, punctuation, and spelling

How Will This Book Help You on Writing Tests?

Writing tests can seem scary if you are not prepared. Fortunately, this book will help you get ready to write your best essays. You will:

● learn what goes into different types of essays

● learn how to read essay prompts just like the ones you will see on tests

● learn and practice methods for planning an essay

● learn how to look at your essay the way a trained reader would learn how to fix common writing errors

Finally, you will get lots of practice, making you a veteran writer who is prepared for any writing test.

WRITING FOR AN ESSAY TEST

Introduction

A writing test asks a student to write an essay or paragraph in response to a written prompt. When you take a writing test, you face the challenge of writing a good essay. Of course, you want to write the best essay possible—and that means having focus, support, and organization.

Focus

An essay should develop a single idea. This idea can be called by several names, including the **focus**, the **central idea**, or the **thesis**. A focus can usually be stated in a single sentence. It might be a point your writing will prove. It can also be a brief statement of what information will be presented in the essay. Think of the focus as a tool that will give direction to your answer on the writing test.

Example Focus:

> **"Installing a traffic light at the corner of First and Lincoln would improve safety in our neighborhood."**

Support

Most of your essay will be made up of statements that support your central idea. These statements can include the following:

- ideas
- evidence
- reasons
- explanations
- examples
- details

All of these together are called the **support**. No matter what form it takes, the support in a writing-test response develops the focus.

Example Supporting Reason:

> **"The corner is dangerous because traffic flow has increased sharply."**

Organization

Clear organization helps your readers understand what you are saying. For instance, suppose you are writing a test response. If your information is not in a reasonable order, the reader will be confused.

Whenever you take an essay test, make sure that you organize your response. You should have an introduction, a body, and a conclusion. Your introduction will introduce your focus. The body of your writing will contain the support. Your conclusion will restate your focus and sum up the main points of the support. In longer essays, the introduction and conclusion will each take a paragraph.

Each supporting point might have its own paragraph. Sometimes your answer may be only a few sentences long, but it should still be organized into an introduction, a body, and a conclusion.

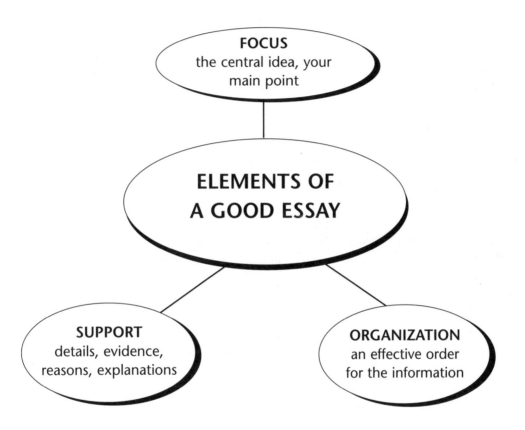

Doing well on a writing test is a matter of finding your focus, supporting your central idea, and organizing your information clearly. Once you have mastered focus, support, and organization, you will be well on your way to mastering the challenge of essay tests.

Focusing Your Essay

Writing a well-focused essay will help you do well on any writing test. Focusing your essay means that everything you include in the essay must relate to your central idea, or focus. No matter what type of essay you write for the test, keep these things in mind while deciding on your focus:

- Your central idea or focus must respond to the prompt.

- Your focus must not be too vague or too specific.

- Limit your focus to one sentence and place that sentence near the end of your introduction.

- Once you have picked a focus, make sure that everything you include in your essay relates to it.

Getting Started

Read the following prompt and the focus sentences below it. Then, choose the focus that best responds to the prompt. Be ready to explain your choice.

> **Prompt**
>
> Many people have places that they consider to be special to them. Write a short essay about your favorite place. First describe the place and then explain why you like it.

Sample Focuses

1. I love to spend time with my friends and family collecting seashells, swimming, and fishing.

2. I would like to go to the mountains for a vacation.

3. Beaches are fun.

4. My best friend and I go to the pool together on weekends.

5. The beach by my house is my favorite place to spend time with family and friends.

Looking It Over

Now take the sentences that you did not choose and rewrite them. Make them focus sentences that could be used for the essay about the writer's favorite place.

1. _____

_____

2. _____

_____

3. _____

_____

4. _____

_____

Trying It Out

Choose one of the following prompts and write a focus sentence that answers it.

Prompt A The principal of your school is considering a dress code that would require students to wear uniforms to school. Many students are on both sides of the issue. Write an essay in which you persuade the principal to agree with your opinion.

Prompt B Many students have a favorite grade or year in school. Write a short essay about your favorite grade or year in school and explain why it is your favorite.

Your Focus:

_____

_____

_____

Supporting the Central Idea

Even the best focus will not earn you a good score on a writing test if it is not supported. After stating your focus in the introduction, you must develop and support it in the body of your essay. Each body paragraph should begin with a topic sentence to introduce the support that follows it. This support can take many forms, depending on the type of essay you are writing. Some kinds of support you will want to use in your writing test include the following:

- ideas
- evidence
- examples
- details
- reasons
- explanations

Remember that a strong essay needs to be focused and well supported. So, while choosing a focus, make sure that you will be able to support it. In other words, write about what you know.

Getting Started

Read the prompt and focus below. Then, read the topic sentences for the body paragraphs of the essay. Circle the number in front of each sentence that supports the central idea.

> **Prompt** Sometimes you have a day in which everything seems to go wrong. Tell about a time you worked hard on something, but it just did not work out.

Sample Focus

We had worked long and hard preparing for the French Club's annual bake sale, but when the big day finally arrived, everything went wrong.

Sample Topic Sentences

1. While walking in the door, I dropped the chocolate cake I had baked for the sale.

2. Few people came to the sale because the posters had the wrong date on them.

3. The French Club wanted to raise funds for educational field trips.

4. We also raised two hundred dollars with a car wash this year.

5. Many French Club members did not attend the sale because of schedule conflicts.

6. On the way to the bank, the club's treasurer lost the money we had earned.

7. The day of the bake sale my alarm didn't go off, and I overslept.

8. My neighbor was an excellent cook who enjoyed baking bread, cakes, and pies.

Looking It Over

Now, using three of the sentences that you chose in the previous activity, fill in the following graphic organizer.

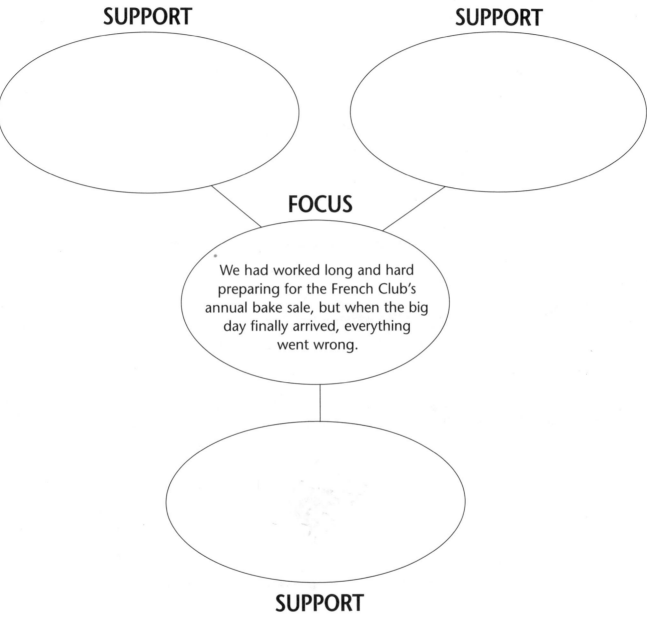

SUPPORT

SUPPORT

FOCUS

We had worked long and hard preparing for the French Club's annual bake sale, but when the big day finally arrived, everything went wrong.

SUPPORT

Trying It Out

Read the following prompt. Then, write a focus and three supporting sentences on your own paper.

Prompt Your school is accepting nominations for Teacher of the Year. You have decided to nominate one of your teachers. Write a focus and three supporting topic sentences explaining why your teacher should win the award.

Organizing Your Essay

Once you have narrowed your essay's focus and gathered your support, you need to think about **organization.** The essay's organization is the way its ideas and information are presented. An essay is usually organized in three parts that fall in is order:

- The **introduction** is a paragraph that catches the reader's attention and states the focus of the essay.

- The **body** is one or more paragraphs that contain the essay's support and details.

- The **conclusion** is a paragraph that restates the essay's focus and sums up the main points.

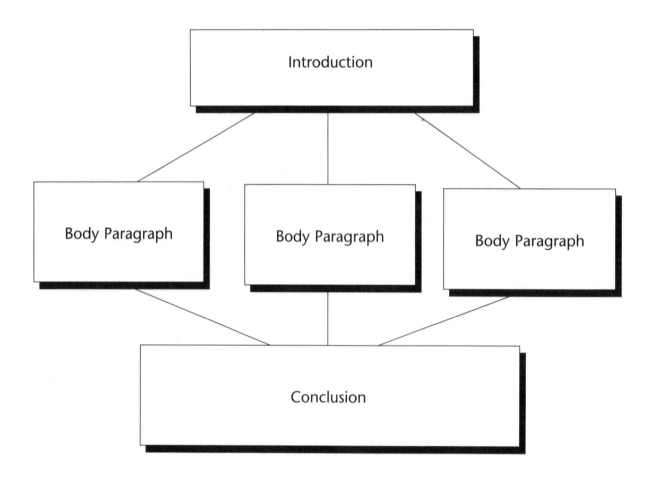

Getting Started

Read the prompt below and the essay on the next page. Look for ways to improve the essay's organization. Then answer the questions.

Prompt) Travel can be an important part of people's lives. Think about a trip that you have made. It does not have to be a long trip. Your trip can be as short as a drive to a nearby town or a visit with a neighbor. Choose a favorite trip you have made, and explain why it was important to you.

My Most Important Trip
by Arturo Mendez

A

When my mom and dad said we were going to the library, I wasn't sure what | 1
that meant. I was only five, and I had not been many places away from home. | 2
As we pulled up to the library, I thought it was the biggest building I had ever | 3
seen. It is only three stories high, but to me it looked like a towering skyscraper. | 4

B

I haven't made any long journeys to faraway places. That doesn't mean that I | 5
haven't made any important trips, though. For instance, a trip to the city library | 6
when I was five has a permanent effect on my life. | 7

C

The inside of the library was even more astounding to me. I had never | 8
imagined that there were so many books in the world! Shelf after shelf rose | 9
high over my head. I felt a little lost and afraid. My dad took my hand and led | 10
me to the children's section. There were bright posters on the walls, and all of | 11
the shelves were within my reach. I pulled out a book. Flipping through the | 12
pages, I admired the colorful pictures and said aloud the words that I knew. I | 13
grabbed a couple more books and found a table and chair just my size. I sat | 14
down to look at these marvelous books. | 15

D

The distance you cover in order to make a trip has nothing to do with its | 16
importance. Your own town could hold places that change you forever. I went | 17
with my parents to a brand-new place and found a lifelong interest. My trip to | 18
the library only took me downtown, but it has lasted my entire life. | 19

E

It seemed just a few minutes before my mom said it was time to go. I was all | 20
ready to throw a world-class fit. Then she told me I could take some books with | 21
me. Imagine! I could take some of these marvelous creations to my house to | 22
enjoy. As we checked them out, she explained that we would bring these books | 23
back and get new ones. I thought that was a great idea. I still do. Since that first | 24
visit, I have made regular trips to the library to trade in old treasures for new. | 25

Looking It Over

Answer these questions on a separate sheet of paper.

1. Which paragraph states the essay's focus? Write this idea in your own words.

2. In lines 8–15, Arturo describes the inside of the library and the impression it made on him. How does this support the focus?

3. List three details or ideas from the essay that support the idea that Arturo's trip to the library was important.

4. How do the sentences in lines 16–19 restate the essay's focus and sum up its main points?

5. Write the paragraph letters in the correct order, with the introduction first and the conclusion last.

Writing on Your Own

Now that you know the basic elements of a good essay, it is time to practice what you have learned. In this lesson, you will go step by step through the process of writing an essay. You will need your own paper for this lesson.

Getting Started

1. **Reading the Prompt:** Writing a test essay begins with carefully reading the prompt.

- Read the entire prompt twice.

- Underline key words, such as **describe**, **explain**, **compare**, **tell**, or **persuade**.

Now, use these two steps with the following prompt.

> **Prompt** Although many students in the United States work during high school, it is not common in other countries. A student from Chile who is spending a year at your high school asks you why so many students in the United States have jobs. Write an essay explaining the advantages and disadvantages of having a job while in high school.

2. **Brainstorming:** Now that you have read the prompt twice and underlined the key parts, you are ready to move on to the next step: brainstorming. At this stage, try to come up with as many ideas as you can. For this essay, separate your ideas under headings called **advantages** and **disadvantages.** Complete the following chart with your ideas. Use additional paper if you need to.

Advantages	Disadvantages
extra money	less study time

Now, go through your list and think about each item. Select either three advantages or three disadvantages that you will be able to support fully. A strong essay is one that is focused and supported, so make sure to choose only ideas that you can develop.

3. Writing the Focus: After you have finished selecting the best ideas from your list of advantages and disadvantages, you can begin working on your focus.

Keep these things in mind when working on your focus:

- The focus should respond to the prompt.

- The focus should be one sentence.

Think of how you want to discuss working in high school. Did you find more advantages than disadvantages, or vice versa? If you think that working in high school is a good idea, a possible focus might be something like the following:

Sample Focus

Working while in high school can take time away from studying, but a job can provide extra income and experience, and encourage responsibility.

Now, write your focus on your own paper.

4. Supporting the Central Idea: After you have your focus, you can start working on your essay. One way to do this is to make an outline and start filling it in.

Sample Outline

Focus: Working while in high school can take time away from studying, but a job can provide extra income and experience, and encourage responsibility.

   I. earn extra income
      A. earn money for entertainment
      B. save up for college or to buy a car
  II. gain experience
      A. see what the workplace is like
      B. try out different kinds of jobs
 III. learn responsibility
      A. learn to be on time; be dependable
      B. work with others

On a separate sheet of paper, make your own outline following the sample given above. Remember that your examples must support the focus. Do not include any details that do not relate to your focus.

5. Writing a First Draft: Using your outline, write a draft of your essay on a separate sheet of paper.

- Write the main body paragraphs first.

- Then, go back and write your introduction and conclusion.

- Be sure to state your focus in the introduction and restate it in the conclusion.

- Make sure you have the paragraphs in a logical order.

- Read it over, checking for correct spelling and punctuation.

Grading an Essay

Knowing how your writing will be scored can help you on a test. Once you have a clear idea of what the graders will be looking for, you can work on improving those aspects of your writing.

Your writing test will be scored by a reader who is trained to evaluate writing. This reader will grade your essay based on a **rubric**. The rubric will set standards for elements such as focus, support, and organization. It will serve as a checklist for clarity, punctuation, and spelling. In this lesson you will practice using rubrics to score writing. Then, you will apply a rubric to your own essay that you wrote in Lesson 4.

Getting Started

Read the prompt and the two introductions written in response to it.

Prompt Write an essay about an event in your life that taught you something about yourself or another person. Describe the event and what you learned as a result.

Sample Introduction A

Have you ever taken a job only to realize that you are in way over your head? Well, I did, and it was an eye-opening experience for me. Our next-door neighbor, Mrs. Schwartz, had hired me to babysit her two-year-old twins one afternoon when I was fourteen years old. Babysitting the twins was by far the hardest job I have ever had.

Sample Introduction B

One summer I went on a hike with my family when we became lost in a heavy fog. It started to get dark, and the temperature began to drop. Finally, I spotted the trail near a tree that had been struck by lightning. Finding the way back from Moosehead Mesa helped me see that I was observant and calm under stress.

Looking It Over

Apply the rubric below to the two introductions. Rate each item on a scale from one to five, five being the best.

Rubric	Sample A Score	Sample B Score
The introduction catches the reader's attention.		
The introduction leads into the topic.		
The introduction states the focus.		
The focus is clear, and it is neither too specific nor too vague.		

Trying It Out

You have now practiced using rubrics to score writing. Apply this rubric to the essay you wrote for Lesson 4 on page 17.

Rubric	Score (1–5)
The introduction catches the reader's attention.	
The introduction leads into the topic and states the focus.	
The focus is clear, and it is neither too specific nor too vague.	
Each body paragraph has a clear main idea that supports the focus.	
Each body paragraph supports its main idea.	
The body paragraphs are in an order that makes sense.	
The conclusion restates the main idea.	
The essay follows the rules of grammar, punctuation, and spelling.	

CHAPTER 1 REVIEW

In this chapter, you have learned the basic elements of a good essay—focus, support, and organization. Understanding these concepts will improve your writing and your writing test scores.

Looking Back

Answer the following questions to review what you have learned in this chapter.

1. What is a focus? How long should a focus be?

   _____

2. Which part of an essay should state the focus? Which part should restate the focus?

   _____

3. What sorts of things make up support?

   _____

4. Where should support appear in an essay?

   _____

5. What is a prompt?

   _____

6. Why is it important to organize an essay?

   _____

Trying It Out

On a separate sheet of paper, respond to the following prompt. Be sure to keep in mind focus, support, and organization as you develop your essay. When you have finished writing your essay, score it by using the rubric on page 19.

(**Prompt**) Choose a favorite book, play, or movie, and think about why you like it. Write an essay telling why you like it and what you learned from reading or seeing it.

STEPS IN PLANNING YOUR ESSAY
Introduction

One key to doing well on a writing test is to plan your answer before you begin writing. The main steps in planning are as follows:

- reading the prompt
- gathering your thoughts
- highlighting the central idea
- organizing your support ideas

Reading the Prompt

If you read the prompt carefully, you will know what kind of information to give in your answer. For example, you might need to tell how two things are different. Or you might tell how they are the same. What kind of information you give depends on the words used in the prompt.

Gathering Your Thoughts

This means writing down the statements you plan to include in your answer. You may write down facts, examples, reasons, and other kinds of statements. While you are planning, you may write these down in any order.

Highlighting the Central Idea

Here, you choose one idea around which to build your answer. This idea will be the focus of your essay.

Organizing Your Support Ideas

The final planning step is organizing your support ideas. You decide in what order you will present the statements that support your central idea.

When you have planned your essay step by step, you will be ready to write a thorough, well-organized answer.

Reading the Prompt

The first step in planning a good essay is reading the prompt carefully. Read the prompt slowly, and read it at least two times.

As you read the prompt, try to the answer these questions:

● What **topic,** or subject, does the prompt ask me to write about? (The prompt below asks you to write about the topic of **a new national holiday.**)

● Who will read my essay? (The prompt below says to write for a **senator.** The senator is your **audience.** If the prompt does not name an audience, you should write to a **general audience.** A general audience is anyone who might be interested in the topic of your essay.)

● What **kind of information** does the prompt ask for? This is sometimes called the **purpose.** (The prompt below asks for the **name of the holiday.** The prompt also asks **why Americans should celebrate it.**)

(**Prompt**) If the United States were to add a new national holiday, what do you think it should be? In an essay addressed to a senator, name the new holiday, and explain why Americans should celebrate it.

Getting Started

Read the following prompts carefully. Then answer the questions.

(**Prompt A**)
For a friend, summarize a book that you remember well.

(**Prompt B**) Think back to when you attended grade school. For a pen pal in a foreign country, compare and contrast your school day now with your school day in grade school.

(**Prompt C**) Describe a time when you experienced severe weather (a big storm, heat wave, or other weather event).

(**Prompt D**) If you could take a trip anywhere, where would you go and why? Be sure to give good reasons in an essay addressed to your teacher.

Looking It Over

Answer the questions about the prompts in **Getting Started** on page 22.

1. What is the topic of prompt A?

    _____

2. Who is the audience in prompt A?

    _____

3. What kind of information is asked for in prompt A?

    _____

4. What is the topic of prompt B?

    _____

5. Who is the audience in prompt B?

    _____

6. What kind of information is asked for in prompt B?

    _____

7. What is the topic of prompt C?

    _____

8. Who is the audience in prompt C?

    _____

9. What kind of information is asked for in prompt C?

    _____

10. What is the topic of prompt D?

    _____

11. Who is the audience in prompt D?

    _____

12. What kind of information is asked for in prompt D?

    _____

Gathering Your Thoughts

Once you understand the prompt, you can start gathering your thoughts. You know you need to supply a **topic,** or subject. One effective way to begin developing topic ideas is by **prewriting.** When you prewrite for a writing test, you set a time limit and come up with as many ideas as you can.

- **Brainstorming** or **freewriting**—First, begin by writing down the topic of the prompt. Then, write down any topic ideas that come into your mind—even ideas that do not make sense. Sentence structure and punctuation do not need to be perfect. No one will see your work. You are only writing to come up with ideas.

- **Making a cluster diagram**—Write all your thoughts in clusters of circles connected by lines. If your topic was "favorite movies," you would write this topic in a circle in the middle of your paper. Around that circle, you would draw other circles for each of your ideas and draw lines connecting them to the center circle.

Getting Started

Read the prompt below, and study the freewriting list and cluster diagram carefully. Remember that the writer will choose one focus idea from his or her freewriting or cluster diagram for the essay.

Prompt) Name a skill you would like to learn. Write an essay telling why the idea of learning this skill appeals to you.

Kristos Opspaulos's Freewriting
Topic: A skill I want to learn

Skills, skills, skills. I don't want to learn anything new. I already know how to read. Okay. I know how to wash the dishes already Wish I didn't. Guitar. I would like that. What else, what else. Hmmmmm. Okay, think. What about making movies? That would be cool. Is that a skill? I think so. Could be a director or an actor or a camera person. Acting would be fun, too. Even in plays. That's something I really want to do. I could act in all kinds of parts. It seems a lot like just playing with friends and I would get to clown around on stage. I suppose I could do that with guitar too but not as much. Clapping and cheering with both. That would be great. Acting—pretend to be someone else.

Kristos Opspaulos's Cluster Diagram

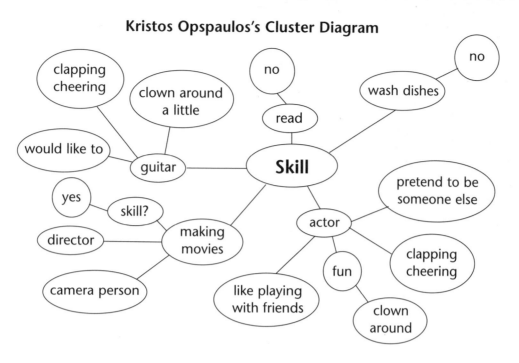

Looking It Over

Now, take a look at Kristos' freewriting and cluster diagram samples. Answer the following questions.

1. Which topic do you think Kristos should select? Explain your answer.

   _____

   _____

2. Choose two topics that Kristos should delete, and tell why he should cut these topics.

   _____

   _____

3. What advantages does a cluster diagram have over freewriting?

   _____

   _____

4. What advantages does freewriting have over a cluster diagram?

   _____

   _____

Trying It Out

Now try prewriting on your own. You can freewrite or make a cluster diagram in order to come up with topic ideas for the following prompt. Use the space on this page. Do not forget to set a time limit of about five minutes.

Prompt Imagine that you wake up tomorrow and there is no longer any electronic entertainment—no more televisions, movies, video games, computers, or recorded music. How would you entertain yourself? How would your life change from day to day? Would your life change for the better or for the worse? Write an essay that tells the story of a day in your life after such a change.

Highlighting the Central Idea

You have already learned how to use brainstorming to develop responses to a prompt. Now you will learn how to build your essay around your strongest idea.

This idea will be the **central idea,** or **focus.** It is a sentence that gives a direct answer to the prompt. The focus is usually placed at the end of the introductory paragraph of the essay. It contains the main idea that the rest of the essay will discuss. You can even think of the focus sentence as a guide for the rest of the essay. Everything you write should be related to the focus.

Look at the following prompt and focus sentences:

Prompt It seems like fewer and fewer schools value arts education—theatre, visual art, dance, and music. Many people believe that the arts are an important part of overall education. However, many schools have cut arts budgets or removed arts programs. Instead, these schools favor academics or sports. Write an essay stating and defending your position on this issue.

Sample Focus A

Arts education should be supported because it teaches students creative thinking, which is a skill they need.

Sample Focus B

Arts education should be supported because it is really great, everyone likes it, and it is not a waste of money like football.

Focus A is a strong answer to the prompt for the following reasons:

- It clearly states the focus of the essay.
- It responds to all parts of the prompt.
- It is not too narrow or too broad.
- It reduces all important information into one sentence.

Focus B is weaker for the following reasons:

- The explanation "because it is really great" is too broad.
- The focus repeats itself.
- The writer assumes that football is a waste of money.

Getting Started

Now, try looking at some focus sentences yourself. Read the prompt and the following focus sentences carefully. Remember all the traits of a good focus sentence.

(**Prompt**) Some people suggest that, in the future, all textbook materials could be found on the Web. Schools would supply students with laptop computers, Internet access, and computer training rather than books. What would a change like this mean to students?

Sample Focus Sentences

A. If our school changed to computerized textbooks, students could keep up with their class materials more easily, but carrying a computer is a big responsibility.

B. Schools should not switch to computers because there are many potential problems that might keep students from completing their assignments on time.

C. Computerized textbooks will create many advantages for students and teachers.

D. It would be difficult for schools to be able to afford to give every student a laptop.

E. Students will be able to complete all their reading using computers.

F. Students who had computerized textbooks could learn more because if they found a textbook subject interesting, they would be more likely to look for more information about it when they are already connected to the Web.

Looking It Over

Answer these questions about the sample focus sentences. Use your own paper to continue your answers if you need more space.

1. Which sample focuses do you think are the strongest and why?

   _____

2. Which sample focuses do not answer the question the prompt asks?

   _____

3. Is focus E a strong answer to the prompt? Explain your answer.

   _____

4. Rewrite answer C. Add the missing parts that would make it a strong focus.

   _____

5. Write your own sample focus to respond to the prompt.

   _____

Trying It Out

Read the prompts below and respond to one. Use the space below or your own paper to brainstorm. Then, write a focus for one of the prompts.

Prompt A

Sometimes we resemble our relatives in the way we look, and sometimes in our personalities. Which of your relatives has a personality most like your own? Write a story that tells about a time you found out the two of you were similar.

Prompt B

Write an essay describing an interesting dream you had. Use details to bring the dream to life for your readers.

Prompt C

Are you shy or outgoing? Are you friendly or reserved? Write an essay describing how you relate to people and how this affects your life.

Your Focus:

_____

_____

_____

_____

Organizing Your Support Ideas

During the prewriting stage, you will begin to notice that some of your ideas fit together. Some of them may not fit at all. Organizing your ideas means putting those ideas into an order that makes sense. How you organize your ideas depends on your purpose. Different types of essays call for different ways to organize. There are four main types of order.

- **Chronological Order** is often used to narrate (tell stories) or to explain the steps in how to do something. Writers use this type of order when they want to describe events in the order in which they happened. Chronological order would be good way to tell how to make a grilled cheese sandwich.

- **Order of Importance** can be used to persuade, describe, explain, or inform. Writers use this order when they want to put their ideas in order from least important to most important, or vice versa. Order of importance would be a good order for reasons why the reader should vote for a candidate.

- **Spatial Order** is used to describe. Writers use this order when they want to show the arrangement of a place, a room, or an object. You can describe a room from left to right, front to back, or even near to far.

- **Logical Order** can be used to define, explain, or compare. Writers use this order when they want to group related ideas together. Logical order would be a good way to organize an essay about different kinds of restaurants.

Getting Started

Now, how do you decide which type of order is the best order for your writing purpose? There are two things you can do to start organizing your ideas: make a chart or use a diagram.

When you make a chart, you decide which ideas or details from your prewriting notes belong together. Your focus will appear at the top of the chart or diagram, and a paragraph topic will appear at the top of each column. Each column will contain details related to the paragraph topic. Look at the prompt and chart on the next page.

Prompt Write an essay describing teenagers. Tell an audience of adults what they most need to know about teens.

Abbey's Chart

Focus: Even though many adults believe teenagers are difficult and create problems, many teenagers have a lot to contribute to the community.		
lots of good teens	positive attitude	unique style
not everyone is in trouble all the time teens help out and volunteer in the community work hard at school, and some hold down jobs, too	very positive about their futures bring a lot of enthusiasm to their work believe they can make a different in the world	teenagers are creative lots of new ideas about how to do things room for many different kinds of expression open to new experience

You can also use a diagram to organize your ideas. Most diagrams use circles or squares to show how ideas are connected. Look at the following prompt and diagram.

Prompt Should teenagers hold down jobs while they are in school? Write an essay persuading readers to agree with your opinion on this issue.

Satish's Diagram

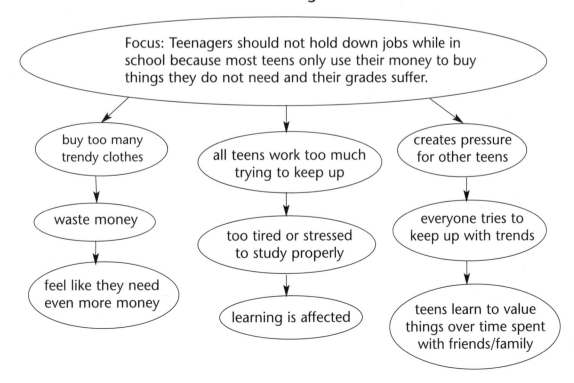

Focus: Teenagers should not hold down jobs while in school because most teens only use their money to buy things they do not need and their grades suffer.

buy too many trendy clothes → waste money → feel like they need even more money

all teens work too much trying to keep up → too tired or stressed to study properly → learning is affected

creates pressure for other teens → everyone tries to keep up with trends → teens learn to value things over time spent with friends/family

Looking It Over

Answer the following questions in the space provided.

1. How are Abbey's chart and Satish's diagram similar?

   _____

   _____

2. How are the chart and the diagram different?

   _____

   _____

3. How do charts and diagrams help put information in order?

   _____

   _____

4. Imagine that Satish wants to put his diagram into chronological order. How should he order his paragraphs?

   _____

   _____

5. What order would you use for the information in Abbey's chart?

   _____

   Place numbers beside the column titles to put her columns in the order your chose.

   _____ lots of good teens

   _____ positive attitude

   _____ unique style

Trying It Out

Choose **one** of the following prompts. Organize your ideas in a chart or diagram. Use the space below to create your chart or diagram.

Prompt A If you could advise new students of the most important things they should know about your school and about other students, what would you tell them? Write an essay describing what this new student most needs to know about your school.

Prompt B Write an essay about a subject that you believe should be studied in school, but is not. Tell readers about the subject, and convince them that it should be added.

LESSON 5

Writing on Your Own

When you are taking a test in which you must write an essay, where do you begin? Usually, the prompt is the best place to start.

In Lesson 1 of this chapter, you learned how to read a prompt, so you already know that you can use a prompt to identify the topic, audience, and purpose. Here is a quick review.

● Topic—what the prompt asks you to write about

● Audience—whom the prompt asks you to write for

● Purpose—what the prompt asks you to do

Read the prompts below, and follow the steps to write your own essay about one of them.

Prompt A (Informative)

Imagine the room of your dreams. What would it contain? What would it look like? How would it be uniquely your own? Write an essay addressed to an audience of your peers describing the room of your dreams.

Prompt B (Narrative)

Can you think of a picture or painting you know well? It could be a famous piece of art or a family photography. Many pictures have a story behind them. Others make people think of stories. Create a story based on real events in your or someone else's life. Write an essay that tells your story to readers.

Step 1. Decide which prompt you will use. Then, on your own paper, write down the topic, audience, and purpose of an essay that responds to the prompt you chose.

Step 2. Use one of the prewriting methods you learned in Lesson 2 to gather ideas for your essay.

Step 3. Look at your prewriting, and find a focus for your essay. Review Lesson 3 if necessary.

Step 4. Use one of the organizational methods you learned in Lesson 4 to order your essay's paragraphs.

Step 5. Write your essay on a separate sheet of paper.

Evaluating Your Writing

Evaluating your writing means judging what you have written and improving weaknesses. People who score tests will go over your writing closely. In this lesson, you will learn to see what these people are trained to see. If you look for the same things in your own writing, you can improve your scores on writing tests.

Getting Started

The person who scores your essay will make sure you have included the following things:

● A clear focus—your central idea must be stated clearly and completely

● Logical organization—your ideas should be organized in a manner that makes sense

● Good development—your ideas must be supported with strong, specific details

The person who scores your essay will use a **rubric** to evaluate your writing. A rubric is a checklist containing key elements that should be included in every essay. You can also use a rubric to judge and improve your own essay.

Trying It Out

Here are rubrics for two different kinds of essays. Use one of the rubrics to evaluate your essay from Lesson 5. If you answered Prompt A, use Rubric A. If you answered Prompt B, use Rubric B. Rate your writing from 1 to 5, using 5 as the highest and 1 as the lowest score.

Rubric (Prompt A)	Rubric for Informative Writing	Score (1–5)
Introductory paragraph	The focus is clear.	
	The writing catches the reader's attention	
Body paragraph	The writer's ideas are logically connected and organized.	
	The writer uses specific details and vivid language to create pictures of people, places, and actions.	
	The setting is described clearly.	
	Characteristics are realistic.	
Concluding paragraph	The meaning of the experience is clear.	
	The story has a clear ending and does not trail off.	
Entire essay	Grammar, spelling, and punctuation are correct.	

Rubric (Prompt B)	Rubric for Narrative Writing	Score (1–5)
Introductory paragraph	The focus is clear.	
	The writing catches the reader's attention	
Body paragraph	The writer's ideas are logically connected and organized.	
	The writer uses specific details and vivid language to create pictures of people, places, and actions.	
	The setting is described clearly.	
	Characteristics are realistic.	
Concluding paragraph	The meaning of the experience is clear.	
	The story has a clear ending and does not trail off.	
Entire essay	Grammar, spelling, and punctuation are correct.	

Looking It Over

After you evaluate your essay, answer the following questions.

1. What are the strongest parts of your essay?

   _____

   _____

2. What are the weakest parts of your essay? Suggest ways you could improve them.

   _____

   _____

3. Choose the weakest part of your essay. Rewrite this problem area to make it stronger.

   _____

   _____

   _____

4. After evaluating your own essay, what would you add to this rubric for your own use?

   _____

   _____

CHAPTER 2 REVIEW

In this chapter, you learned the steps necessary to planning an essay. You have learned to write a focused, organized essay. You have also learned how to judge the quality of your essay.

Looking Back

Answer these questions in the space provided.

1. What three things should you look for in a writing prompt?

   _____

2. What are two prewriting methods you can use to gather your thoughts?

   _____

3. What should your focus tell your readers?

   _____

   _____

4. How should you decide what your focus will be?

   _____

5. What are four ways you can organize your essay?

   _____

   _____

6. What should you look back at as you write your essay?

   _____

7. What are three things you should look for when evaluating your writing?

   _____

   _____

Trying It Out

Respond to the prompt below on your own paper.

Prompt Many parents pressure their children to go into certain career fields. How does this pressure affect teens who want to follow different career paths? Is the pressure helpful or harmful? Write an essay addressed to the parents of teenagers in which you state and defend your opinion on the issue.

DIFFERENT TYPES OF ESSAYS

Introduction

You have learned many skills for writing. Now let's look at some different kinds of writing. Each of the four types of essays has a different purpose and can be organized in a different way.

Expository Essay

An expository essay gives information with supporting statements for each main point. This essay may even look like a report and is often the basis for a business letter. A good way to organize this kind of essay is with a list. An essay explaining what makes a good student would be an expository essay.

Persuasive Essay

A persuasive essay takes a side in an argument and shows why that side is correct. The prompt may ask you to write a letter or a speech instead of an essay. A good way to organize the arguments for this essay is to have two columns. One is for pros, and the other is for cons. An essay urging students to recycle would be a persuasive essay.

Narrative Essay

A narrative essay tells a story. The prompt may be a few sentences or a picture. One way to organize a narrative essay is with a story web detailing the characters, setting, events, and conclusion. An essay that tells about something interesting you did last year would be a narrative essay.

Descriptive Essay

A descriptive essay gives the reader a visual image and a feeling for something described. The prompt is sometimes a picture. You can easily organize this kind of essay with a numbered list to keep your description orderly. An essay telling what your school is like would be a descriptive essay.

The elements of focus, support, and organization are necessary in each type of essay. Note the things that make the essays different, and practice using them. Assume that your audience has never heard of your subject. You must lead them to your main idea carefully and give them plenty of supporting details.

Description of Different Types of Essays

You write an **expository essay** to explain. You could be writing to tell differences and similarities, to give results or facts, or to define. Parts of the expository essay are as follows:

- **Introductory paragraph** with a clear focus sentence. You should mention your main points. This way you are telling the reader ahead of time what you will explain.

- **Body** consisting of one paragraph for each main point. Supporting statements in body paragraphs should have good, solid facts.

- **Concluding paragraph** that restates your focus. Do not use the same words that you used in the first paragraph. Reword your focus. The last paragraph is not the place to put new ideas.

Expository Prompt

What new activity, sport, or hobby would you like to learn more about? Explain your choice.

You write a **persuasive essay** to tell people why they should do something or why they should agree with you. You take a side in an argument and defend it. Parts of the persuasive essay are as follows:

- **Introductory paragraph** with a clear focus stating your opinion. You must choose a side in the argument and state what it is.

- **Body** consisting of two or more paragraphs. In some paragraphs give the pros, or positives, that support your opinion. In some give the cons, or opposite opinions, and tell why they are wrong or why you do not agree with them.

- **Concluding paragraph** that restates, or rewords, your opinion and reminds the reader of your pros. The last paragraph is not the place to put new ideas.

Persuasive Prompt

In some towns, officials want to make a law against the use of any kind of electronic machine (cell-phone, two-way radio, CD player) while driving. People feel that these machines distract drivers. Consider the pros and cons of the new law. In an essay, convince the city board to vote either yes or no on this new law.

A **narrative essay** is basically a story. The story could be based on real people or events, on your life, or on your imagination. Parts of the narrative essay are as follows:

- **Introductory paragraph** with a setting, introduction of characters, background information, and the focus of the story.

- **Body** consisting of one or more paragraphs telling what happens. A story often will include dialogue, or characters' exact words.

- **Concluding paragraph** with the ending and a comment or thought for the reader. Sometimes this is a moral. A good story deserves a good ending.

Narrative Prompt Questioning our decisions after an event is normal. People often ask, "Did I do the right thing?" In an essay, tell about an event in which the character—you or an imaginary person—asks this question.

A **descriptive essay** describes a person, an object, or an event. Figurative language, metaphors, and similes are found in this type of essay. Parts of the descriptive essay are as follows:

- **Introductory paragraph** with a clear focus and a general impression of the topic.

- **Body** consisting of one or more paragraphs. These paragraphs give the details about the topic in a logical order (top to bottom, front to back, or beginning to end). Details should include some of the five senses.

- **Concluding paragraph** that restates the focus and gives a strong thought or opinion about the topic.

Descriptive Prompt Imagine that a local charity is putting on a fair. Your friend wants to be a clown for the fair and needs your help. Describe the new clown face you design for your friend.

Looking It Over

You read an essay that tells how an apple looks, feels, smells, and tastes. Which type of essay did you read?

Writing an Expository Essay

When you write a report, tell about a project, or compare and contrast, you are writing an expository essay. A good writer will **hook** the reader into reading the essay by grabbing his or her attention. You can grab the reader's attention at the beginning of the essay by stating a shocking fact or statistic, or by telling a joke. You might begin by asking a question or giving a quotation.

Words that may clue you that the prompt is asking for an expository essay are as follows: **trace, analyze, respond to, clarify, discuss, classify, compare, contrast, define, explain,** or **summarize.**

Getting Started

Read the following prompt, see how the writer organizes her ideas, and read the essay. Then answer the questions.

> **Prompt** As we grow up, we hear sayings from our family and friends. One that is often heard is "A stitch in time saves nine." In an essay, respond to this saying.

Janine organized the essay using a list of possible points. It looked like this:

A Stitch in Time Saves Nine

- it's a wise saying, passed through time with no known origin
- sewing: if you repair a torn seam when it needs one stitch, it won't take 9 stitches or become impossible to fix—example: T-shirt

  or lose a button—example: jacket

- other damaged things: if you repair them at first sign of wear, they need less time, money, or effort

  —example: oil in car

- relationships: if you handle a small problem, it will never get big

  —example: argument with sister

- must be true because it still works. it's about prevention and maintenance, like "Be prepared"?

A Stitch in Time Saves Nine
by Janine Lemond

Did you ever hear the saying "I didn't just fall off the onion truck," or "A   1
watched pot never boils"? Some things that parents and grandparents say   2
make no sense. Sometimes a saying that has no known origin has been passed   3
down through time because it's good. "A stitch in time saves nine" is just such   4
a saying. It is true for sewing, for tools and machines, and even for   5
relationships.   6

It even sounds as though it should work for sewing. When I had a tiny tear in   7
my best blue T-shirt, I thought about mending it. But that meant getting out   8
Mom's sewing kit, and I had other things to do. I threw it in the wash. A week   9
later I wanted to wear it, but the tear was then three inches long. The washer   10
had pulled on it. It took me nine times as long to fix it. The same thing almost   11
happened with my jacket. A button was loose when I put on the jacket, but I   12
went out to play ball anyway. When I got home, the button was gone. I had to   13
buy a new button and sew it on. The button was bright blue, like the jacket.   14

The saying also applies to other things. I remember walking into the kitchen   15
one day to see my mom using a screwdriver on her frying pan. I asked her what   16
she was doing, and she said, "The pan's handle is a little loose. A stitch in time 17
saves nine." What if she hadn't tightened it? The handle could have fallen off   18
while she was moving something hot from the stove! My dad is always   19
checking the oil on his car. I guess preventing a major problem, like the car   20
breaking down, is the same thing.   21

Believe it or not, the saying also works for relationships. My sister and I have   22
been fighting about whose turn it is, who has to watch our little brother, and   23
other things for a long time. Last week we had a big fight about whose turn it   24
was to talk on the telephone. We pulled and pulled on the phone until we   25
broke it. Now, neither of us can use the phone, and we have to wait until we   26
earn some money to replace the telephone. I should have mended that   27
relationship a long time ago.   28

Some old sayings like "A stitch in time saves nine" really are true, wise sayings. 29
They may sound old, but they still work. Maybe this old saying turned into the   30
Boy Scouts' motto, "Be prepared."   31

Looking It Over

Answer the questions below in the space provided.

1. Look at Janine's introductory paragraph. Why does it grab your attention?

   _____

   _____

2. What is Janine's focus? How could it be stated more clearly?

   _____

   _____

3. How does Janine restate her focus in the last paragraph?

   _____

   _____

4. What are Janine's main points?

   _____

   _____

5. Which sentence in lines 7–14 is not related to Janine's topic?

   _____

   _____

Trying It Out

It is now time for you to write an expository essay. Read the prompt below and write an essay that responds to it. Remember to choose a focus, organize your thoughts, and use supporting statements. Write your essay on your own paper.

Prompt A good friend is a treasure each person tries to find. Have you had a really good friend? Explain what a good friend is so that you and others can identify one easily.

Writing a Persuasive Essay

When you convince your friends to play one game rather than another, you are being persuasive. When you write a letter asking students to support a club or cause, you are writing a persuasive essay. A good persuasive writer keeps a reader's thoughts and feelings in mind. Such a writer addresses both the pros and cons of an argument. He or she tells readers the strengths of a position, and addresses possible weaknesses of the position as well. A good persuasive writer convinces readers that his or her position offers the best solution for the problem at hand.

Words that may clue you that a prompt is asking for a persuasive essay are as follows: **agree/disagree, viewpoint, argue/argument, consider, stance, controversy/controversial, should/should not, convince, opinion, debate, issue, oppose, persuade, position,** and **support.**

Getting Started

Read the following prompt and see how the writer organizes her ideas. Then, read the essay, and answer the questions.

> **Prompt** Smoking is a serious problem among teenagers. Some people have suggested laws designed to prevent teens from smoking. These laws take away the drivers license of any teenager who is caught with cigarettes. Do you think this method is a good idea? Write an essay telling whether or not this is a good idea and why.

The writer, who agreed with the method, organized her essay using the following list of pros and cons, reasons people might agree or disagree with her position.

Pros

- drivers license is a sign of adulthood

- drivers need responsibility, but smokers don't have responsibility

- teenagers care about drivers license

Cons

- not fair

- drivers license has nothing to do with cigarettes

A Red Light for Smokers
by Paige Alexander

Despite having many reasons not to smoke, many teenagers choose to start smoking. In order to stop teen smoking, some states take away the drivers license of any teenager caught with cigarettes. Though at first this idea seems unfair, it may be the best way to keep teenagers from smoking. [1] [2] [3] [4]

Some teenagers complain that taking away drivers licenses has nothing to do with smoking. However, if we think about it carefully, we can see that the drivers license has more connection to smoking than most people realize. [5] [6] [7]

First of all, the drivers license is a sign of adulthood. Many teens who smoke do it to look grown-up. When someone is worried about looking mature, there is no better way to punish that person than taking away his or her drivers license. Thus, taking away their licenses is a good way to keep teens from smoking. [8] [9] [10] [11]

Second, young smokers prove that they are not responsible enough to drive. Every teenager knows that smoking kills. Teens who do smoke are not responsible enough to keep themselves safe. How can we trust them to be responsible enough as drivers? [12] [13] [14] [15]

Third, taking away the right to drive is the only thing that will catch a teenager's attention. Teenagers do not care that cigarettes could harm them in thirty years. They do care about whether or not they have the freedom of mobility. They care about whether they can visit their friends at will instead of being stuck at home. [16] [17] [18] [19] [20]

At first, the right to drive legally and the choice to smoke illegally seem to be unrelated. Still, taking away a teen smoker's drivers license is a good way to curb teen smoking for several reasons. Taking driving away from someone shows the world that the person is not grown-up. Also, teens who smoke prove that they are not responsible enough to drive. Finally, threatening a teenager with the loss of his or her right to drive is the most effective way to catch the teen's attention. [21] [22] [23] [24] [25] [26] [27]

Looking It Over

Answer the questions below in the space provided.

1. Look at Paige's introductory paragraph. Is the topic clear?

    _____

2. What opinion is stated in the first paragraph? Is it restated in the last paragraph?

    _____

    _____

3. Which of Paige's arguments is weakest? Why?

    _____

    _____

    _____

4. Describe the audience that Paige is addressing. Explain your answer.

    _____

    _____

    _____

    _____

Trying It Out

It is time for you to write a persuasive essay on your own paper. Remember to make your opinion clear in a focus statement. Organize your thoughts in a list of pros and cons. Dispute the opposite opinion and support your points with examples.

Prompt Should people be allowed to share and trade music over the Internet for free? Some record companies think that sharing music is the same as stealing and that the courts should force people to stop. Decide whether you are for or against the free sharing and trading of music online. In an essay, persuade your reader to agree with you.

Writing a Narrative Essay

When you write in your journal and tell about your day, you are writing a narrative. When you make up a story for your little sister or brother, you are telling a narrative. A narrative is a story. It should be written like a story, with plot, description, and possibly even dialogue between characters. As with other types of essays, you will state the focus or use hints of the central idea in the first paragraph of the narrative essay.

Words that may clue you that the prompt is for a narrative essay are as follows: **relate, remember, narrate, recall, story, tell, event, experience, incident,** and **recount.**

Hint for Narrative Essays: Overuse of any word or phrase such as "suddenly" or "and then" makes the essay boring to the reader.

Getting Started

Read the following prompt. Notice how the writer organizes his ideas. Then, read the essay, and answer the questions.

Prompt People often decide whether they like or dislike something before they know anything about it. Write an essay that relates an event in which a character or characters are surprised to learn they like something after they experience it.

The writer organized the essay using a story web. It looked like this:

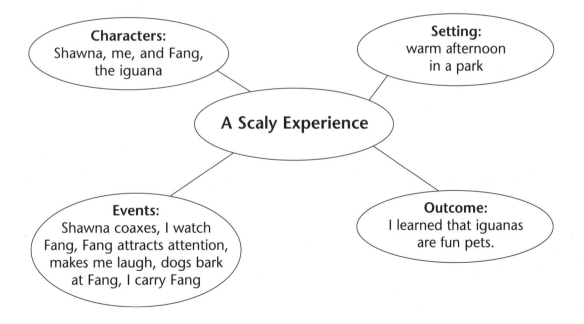

A Scaly Experience
by Mario Alvarez

I always thought that dogs and cats were the only good pets. One afternoon of   1
watching my friend's pet iguana, Fang, changed my mind. Shawna and I were   2
walking her iguana one warm afternoon when we passed a volleyball game.   3
Shawna played volleyball for her high school team. "Come on, Mario," said   4
Shawna. "Watch Fang while I get in on this game of volleyball. You might have   5
fun with Fang if you give him a chance."   6

"No way. Don't make me responsible for that ugly creature. He might attack   7
me or try to eat a cat," I answered.   8

"Oh, Mario, Fang's never hurt anyone. Pleeeeease!" begged Shawna.   9

"Okay, but just this once and you can only play one game," I said.   10

As my friend jogged happily onto the volleyball court, I looked down at the   11
long green lizard on the red leash. I felt silly with such a weird animal. "I bet no   12
one will get near me while I walk this scaly thing around," I thought.   13

Some boys playing Frisbee stared at Fang and began asking several questions   14
about him. Then some joggers stopped to get a closer look. Fang let the   15
curious onlookers touch him and look closely at his green spikes. They liked   16
Fang's twitching tail and funny eyes that seemed to watch them carefully. I   17
laughed at some of Fang's movements. Sometimes, he moved like a human.   18

Before I walked away, some dogs barked at Fang, and one bolted toward us.   19
Fang stretched his leash, scooted up a tree, and hissed until the dogs retreated.   20
Apparently, Fang had an attitude and could take care of himself. To avoid   21
trouble with any other dogs that might come near at any time, I put Fang on   22
my shoulder. I was a little worried that the iguana would rip my shirt or try to   23
bite me. To my surprise, Fang sat calmly on his new perch and seemed to enjoy   24
the ride. More people came up to meet me and Fang, and they all laughed and   25
talked about the interesting pet.   26

Before I realized that any time had passed, the volleyball game was over.   27
Shawna sprinted up to where Fang and I stood. She asked me if I wanted to   28
return her ugly creature.   29

"Okay, you win," I said, reluctant to hand Fang back to her. "Iguanas can be   30
fun. As a matter of fact, I just might get one for myself."   31

Looking It Over

Answer the questions below in the space provided.

1. Look at Mario's introductory paragraph. What is his central idea?

   _____

2. Which sentence in lines 1–6 does not seem to belong? Why?

   _____

   _____

3. How does the dialogue help make the story more interesting?

   _____

   _____

Trying It Out

Read the following prompt and write a narrative essay that responds to it. You will need to use your own paper.

Digital Imagery ©2000 PhotoDisc, Inc.

Prompt An old saying goes, "A picture can tell a thousand words," but those words tell a different story to each person who looks at the picture. Look closely at the picture on this page. What story does it tell you? Use your creativity and personal experience to tell a story about what is happening.

Writing a Descriptive Essay

When you tell a friend how your new outfit looks, you are being descriptive. When you write in your diary about a special dinner you had, you are being descriptive. A good writer will use details to make the reader see, smell, hear, feel, or taste the item being described.

Words that may clue you that the prompt is asking for a descriptive essay are as follows: **express, picture, portray, senses/sensory, convey, depict, describe/description**, or **visualize.**

Getting Started

Read the following prompt, see how the writer organizes her ideas, and read the essay. Then, answer the questions.

> **Prompt** Describe a place where you like to spend time. Do not tell a story about that place. Instead, give the reader a real sense of what the place looks, smells, sounds, feels, and/or tastes like.

The writer decided to write about a movie theater. To get ideas, she made a chart based on the five senses.

sight	smell	sound	feel	taste
dark curtains on walls designed to disappear	strong popcorn sweet sodas and candy	large speakers shake the building	seats too small at first floor sticky from sodas	no particular taste maybe popcorn

The Intriguing Theater
by Laura Sechelski

Many people like places that are beautiful and bright. The smell of flowers in a   1
garden, bright colors in the sunlight, the feel of a gentle breeze—most people   2
look for these things in a place they want to visit, but not me. One of my   3
favorite places to visit is the movie theater. Its unique odors, its darkness, and   4
its cramped feel set it apart from the rest of the world.   5

The first thing that I notice about the movie theater is the smell. Year after year   6
of fake butter on stale popcorn has given the theater an odor that hits my nose   7
the minute I walk through the door. It mingles with the aromas of soda pop,   8
chocolate, and licorice to create a strong buttery-sweet scent which is equal   9
parts appetizing and disgusting.   10

My nose is probably working overtime because there is nothing for my eyes to   11
see. The rest of the theater is dark, even when the lights are on. Huge, dark red   12
curtains clothe the black-painted walls. The chairs are black plastic and metal   13
with dark red cushions. The entire theater is designed to disappear when the   14
lights go out.   15

Walking to my seat, I can feel my sneakers sticking to the floor with every step.   16
At least once in every matinee, someone has spilled a sugary beverage onto the   17
concrete floor beneath the seats. About once every century, the theater workers   18
mop the space under the chairs, so the floor is stickier than fly paper. With each   19
step, I worry about getting stuck. When I finally flop into my seat, it seems too   20
small, and I wonder how I will last an hour and half sitting there. Strangely,   21
once the movie starts I do not even notice how cramped the chair is.   22

The movie theater is like another world, with its own special smells, sights, and   23
sensations. The stale odor, the dark surroundings, and the sticky floor make it a   24
unique environment. I enjoy visiting, but I'm glad not to stay for more than a   25
single movie.   26

Looking It Over

Answer the questions below in the space provided.

1. Read Laura's first paragraph. What is her focus?

   _____

   _____

2. Which senses does Laura's essay appeal to?

   _____

   _____

3. If Laura wanted to write another paragraph, what might it be about?

   _____

   _____

4. Does Laura's conclusion remind you of her focus? If so, how?

   _____

   _____

Trying It Out

Respond to the following prompt with a descriptive essay. Make your focus and topic clear from the start, and organize your essay in a logical way. Describe each aspect of your topic using some of the five senses. Remember to end your essay by reminding your reader of your focus (give an opinion about your topic). Use your own paper.

Prompt Many people pick out cars that show who they are. Describe the car you would like to own. Tell how the car would look, sound, feel, smell, and/or taste.

CHAPTER 3 REVIEW

By now you have practiced writing four types of essays, each with its own purpose and organization. The expository gives information. The persuasive argues for your opinion. The narrative tells a story. Finally, the descriptive describes something in detail. Each type of essay needs a clear focus so readers can understand your purpose. Supporting evidence or details strengthen the essay, and good organization makes it easy to read.

Looking Back

Answer the questions below in the space provided.

1. Name a good way to organize each of the four essay types.

   _____

   _____

2. List the ways a writer can grab the reader's attention at the beginning of an expository essay.

   _____

   _____

3. Which type of prompt may ask for a letter or speech instead of an essay?

   _____

4. List three words that let you know the prompt is for a narrative essay.

   _____

5. What type of details should you use in a descriptive essay?

   _____

Trying It Out

Read the following prompt. Decide which type of essay would best answer the prompt. Then, write an appropriate response on your own paper.

> **Prompt** Your state legislature is voting soon on a new law that will lower highway speeds. Some people feel that this will reduce the number of traffic accidents. Others feel that it will just increase the number of traffic tickets. Decide whether you support or oppose the new law. Write an essay persuading your representative to agree with your opinion on this issue.

WRITING STRATEGIES FOR PROBLEM AREAS

Introduction

When taking a writing test, you must show your command of the English language. To write a good essay, you must pay attention to punctuation, spelling, and other basic language skills.

Sentence Structure

If you are unable to write sentences that express complete thoughts, your reader may not understand what you are trying to say. If you try to say too much in a single sentence, your readers may be confused. Readers are most often confused by sentence fragments and run-on sentences. Luckily, both of these problems are easy to correct.

Punctuation and Capitalization

Using a period when you need a comma can keep your reader from understanding your ideas. Not capitalizing a name can make your writing unclear. Take the time to learn basic rules for commas, semicolons, quotation marks, apostrophes, and capital letters.

Combining Sentences

Saying the same thing over and over will bore your readers. If you notice that you are repeating words or phrases, then combine sentences using modifiers, phrases, or clauses. Always state ideas as clearly and plainly as possible.

Paragraphs and Transitions

Always begin a new paragraph when moving to a new idea or area of support. Using smooth transitions between paragraphs helps keep your reader's attention. Your essay should not "jump around" from topic to topic. The use of paragraphs and transitions will help your overall organization as you support your focus.

Using Words Properly

Misspelled and misused words pull your reader's attention away from your focus. They can even confuse or mislead. Pay special attention to spelling as well as to **homophones**. Homophones are words that sound the same, but have different spellings and meanings.

If you pay attention to your sentences, punctuation, word use, and paragraphs while taking a writing test, your writing will be clearer and easier to follow.

Sentence Structure

As a writer, you must make sure that your sentences are complete and easy to understand. Run-on sentences, which contain too much information and not enough punctuation, can be very confusing. Similarly, every sentence needs a subject telling whom or what the sentence is about. You should also check to see that each sentence has a **predicate**, which includes an action or describes the condition of the subject. When a sentence lacks either a subject or a predicate, it is a sentence fragment.

Run-on Sentences

A **run-on sentence** includes two or more complete sentences written as one sentence. Readers become confused when all this information is given at once without a chance for the reader to pause and absorb it.

Example Run-on Sentence:

Dogs often try to please their masters cats generally please themselves.

Run-on sentences can be corrected in several ways:

- **Form two or more separate sentences from the run-on sentence.**

  Dogs often try to please their masters. Cats generally please themselves.

- **Join the independent clauses with a comma and a coordinating conjunction.**

  Dogs often try to please their masters, but cats generally please themselves.

  Note: The coordinating conjunctions are **and, or, for, nor, but, yet,** and **so.**

- **Join the independent clauses with a semicolon.**

  Dogs often try to please their masters; cats generally please themselves.

- **Turn one of the independent clauses into a subordinate clause by adding a subordinating conjunction or a relative pronoun.**

  Although dogs often try to please their masters, cats generally please themselves.

Sentence Fragments

A **sentence fragment** is a group of words that lacks either a subject or a predicate. It does not express a complete thought.

Example Sentence Fragment:

A new volunteer at the library.

This group of words is about a volunteer, but it does not say what the volunteer is doing or describe the condition of the volunteer. It can be fixed by adding a predicate.

Example Complete Sentence:

A new volunteer at the library found the book I wanted.

As the example shows, fragments often require that the writer add information. However, a fragment can sometimes be repaired by simply connecting it to a nearby sentence.

Example Sentence Fragment:

Music makes me feel mellow. Calms my nerves.

Example Complete Sentence:

Music makes me feel mellow and calms my nerves.

Getting Started

Read the following prompt and essay. Look for run-on sentences and sentence fragments as you read. Then, answer the questions.

(**Prompt**) If your town were building a new high school, for whom should the school be named? Explain why this person deserves such an honor.

Our New High School
by Trang Vo

Public schools are often named for people who have had a great influence on   1
the community. Our school board intends to name our new school for just such   2
an individual. The person who most deserves this honor is known throughout   3
our town for her dedication to learning the new high school should be named   4
after Lena Gaffney.   5

Our high school deserves the name of someone who is a hometown hero.   6
Someone we are proud of. Ms. Gaffney's entire career as a teacher has been   7
spent in our hometown, and most of our residents were at one time her   8
students. She is a living example of a noble life, we are lucky to have her as a   9
citizen of our town.   10

Ms. Gaffney has dedicated her life to public education few students in our town   11
have been untouched by her and the programs she has encouraged. Always   12
willing to go the extra mile. Ms. Gaffney listened to students when they needed   13
help and also shared in their many victories. Both large and small.   14

Even after her retirement ten years ago. Ms. Gaffney has remained active in our   15
schools. She volunteers as a tutor for struggling students. Students know she is   16
always available to share her expertise all they need to do is ask. She still puts 17
students' needs first. I know of no person more deserving of the honor than   18
she is.   19

Looking It Over

1. Lines 6–10 include a sentence fragment and a run-on sentence. Circle both of these problems.

2. Lines 11–14 are almost entirely made up of run-on sentences and sentence fragments. Rewrite the lines, correcting the mistakes. Use your own paper.

3. Circle the run-on sentence in lines 15–19.

4. How do the mistakes in this essay affect your ability to read and understand it easily?

   _____

5. How do the mistakes in this essay hurt the writer's message?

   _____

Capitalization and End Punctuation

When responding to a prompt on a writing test, you should always remember that small mistakes add up. Capitalization errors and incorrect end punctuation are common mistakes. Fortunately, they are easy to avoid.

Capitalization

Most writers have no trouble remembering to capitalize proper nouns, but other capitalization rules may give you trouble. Included are rules you need most often when writing in a test situation.

Things that are ALWAYS Capitalized

- All proper nouns (the names of particular people, places, or things)

  Monday, Thanksgiving, World Series, Evans Junior High, Lake Erie

Things That Are SOMETIMES Capitalized

- A person's title **only** when it is used as a name in direct address or when it comes before a person's name

  What do you think of our plan, **Senator**?

  The **senator** was unhappy with our plan.

  I told **Senator Murphy** about the new plan.

- Words showing a family relationship **only** when they are used as proper names or used as titles

  I asked **Aunt** Ruby for all her baking secrets.

  I asked my **aunt** for all her baking secrets.

Things That Are ALMOST NEVER Capitalized

- Names of seasons (**summer, fall, spring, winter**)
- Names of academic years or terms (**freshman, spring semester**)
- Names of school subjects, **unless** they are language courses or are followed by a course number (**Spanish, chemistry, math, History 101**)
- Compass directions **unless** they name a particular place or region

  Tom asked me to drive **east** for twenty miles.

  Manuela grew up in **the East**.

End Punctuation

Although most writers are familiar with the rules for end punctuation, they often become careless when writing an essay.

- A period is used to end both declarative statements and imperative sentences (commands). Since most sentences end with periods, writers sometimes carelessly end questions with a period. Be careful in your own writing.

- A question mark is used at the end of an interrogative sentence (question). Be sure the sentence is truly a question before using a question mark.

    Is Quinn coming over to study later?

    I asked Quinn if she wanted to study later.

- An exclamation point is used to end an exclamatory sentence. This type of sentence may express a strong feeling or be a forceful command or request.

    I could not believe it!

Getting Started

Circle the capitalization errors, and correct the end punctuation mistakes in the following sentences. Some sentences have more than one error.

1. The police officer instructed me to turn West onto turner street.

2. I wondered why the washington monument was closed to the public?

3. My letter to the Governor was returned without a reply.

4. When did you call your Mother to ask about the Birthday party?

5. The southwest enjoys warm weather most of the year.

6. My brother will attend lakeview high school this Fall.

7. When my Uncle called us, I asked him where he was?

8. The bridge across the Red river was closed on thursday.

Looking It Over

Read the following prompt and paragraph. Look for errors in capitalization and end punctuation as you read. Then, answer the questions.

> **Prompt** Think about the people who have been influential in your life. Choose a person who has made a difference to you, and explain how this person has affected you.

One Paragraph from Sample Essay

Mr. Franklin's Influence

Mr. Franklin challenged his students to go beyond what was expected. When he announced that the first-semester assignment was an eight-page research paper, I thought, "Is he crazy." However, I decided that I would work a little bit every day. I even asked if I could do a little bit of Extra Credit work so that I could raise my grade? I found that the more I did, the more I wanted to do. Soon history was my favorite subject, and I was making higher grades than I ever had before. The Principal even recognized me in a special ceremony for outstanding students. By the Spring semester, I realized that I was actually enjoying my work at school.

1. Circle the sentence that needs a question mark, and rewrite it correctly.

   _____

   _____

   _____

2. Circle the four capitalization errors. Rewrite these words correctly.

   _____

   _____

   _____

3. Circle the other end punctuation error. Rewrite the sentence correctly.

   _____

   _____

   _____

Punctuation

It is very important to use correct punctuation when writing an essay. Punctuation marks are the road signs for your readers, helping them understand how ideas fit together. Improper punctuation can make reading more difficult and even change your meaning.

Commas

When using commas, a good rule to follow is that commas are needed to indicate pauses or to prevent confusion. Some more specific comma rules are listed below.

- Use commas to separate three or more items in a series.

    Juan gave the tickets to **Ahmed, Mary Beth, and Fatima.**

- Use a comma to show a pause after introductory words or phrases.

    After I saw the movie, I walked over to Benny's house.

- Use a comma before a coordinating conjunction (**and, or, for, nor, but, yet,** and **so**) that joins the independent clauses of a compound sentence. Independent clauses are clauses that could stand alone as complete sentences.

    Kenisha wanted to go home, **but** she did not have a ride.

- Use commas to set off words or phrases that are not needed in the sentence and to set off nouns used to address people.

    Mrs. Payne, may I ask a question?

    Our teacher, **who went to Harvard,** assigned too much homework.

    Our standards, **after all,** are very high.

Apostrophes

- Use an apostrophe to show possession.
  - If a noun is singular, ad **'s**, even if the singular noun already ends in **–s.**

    mother**'s** car, George**'s** desk, Mr. Jones**'s** book

  - If a noun is plural and ends with **–s,** just add an apostrophe.

    my parents' car, the girls' ribbons, the Andersons' house

  - If a noun is plural but does not end in **–s,** add **'s.**

    the women**'s** coats, the people**'s** choice

- Use an apostrophe to replace letters or numerals that have been left out of a contraction.

    are not = aren't   I will = I'll   1980 = '80

Quotation Marks

- Use quotation marks at the beginning and end of a quotation to show that you are quoting someone directly or that you are copying words that someone else wrote.

  The police officer said, "May I see your license, please?"

  Note: Commas will often be used to separate words that are quoted from words that are not quoted.

- **Do not** use quotation marks with an indirect quotation (a retelling, in your own words, of what someone else said, thought, or wrote).

  My brother said that he would not attend the club meeting tonight.

- Use quotation marks to set off the title of a short written work, such as a story or song. If you are including the entire work, you do not need to use quotation marks for the title.

  My favorite song is "My Way."

- Use quotation marks to set off words used in unexpected ways, such as nicknames, slang, technical terms, or unusual expressions.

  When my mother was young, her family called lunch "tea."

Semicolons

- Semicolons are mainly used to connect closely related independent clauses that are not joined by a coordinating conjunction. Remember that independent clauses can stand alone as sentences. Fragments and clauses that cannot stand alone cannot be joined using a semicolon.

  Sharks are interesting creatures; however, I still prefer dolphins.

Getting Started

Cross out the words that contain errors, and write the correct words or punctuation above. If there are no punctuation errors, simply write "correct."

1. The twins projects were so well done that they earned full credit.

2. The teacher asked me "If I would help carry the textbooks?"

(continued on next page)

3. Because Dwight won the race he received a gold medal.

4. The dog ran across the road; but he was not injured.

5. Whenever it is convenient for me I help my neighbors son with his math.

6. William asked Do you want to sign up for the election committee?

7. Our science teacher, Mr. Mabry, likes to refer to us as "life-forms."

8. Last night I heard Naomi Shihab Nye read her poem called Late.

Trying It Out

Read the following prompt and the introduction to the essay. Add any missing commas, semicolons, quotation marks, or apostrophes that are needed in this paragraph. Correct any incorrect punctuation. Cross out any unnecessary punctuation marks that have been included.

Prompt Everyone faces difficult tasks that they must overcome. Describe one difficult task that you are proud to have completed.

Sample Introductory Paragraph

Hiking the Grand Canyon

Last summer I did something that I never thought I could do. I hiked to the bottom of the Grand Canyon. As I was walking down the steep trail I thought to myself I can never make it back out of here. I was surprised to find however that I was strong, and determined enough to make it out. My parent's did not need to help me. After that experience I know that I can do anything I put my mind to.

Combining Sentences

Good writers know that it is always best to use as few words as possible to say what needs to be said. When writing an essay, pay attention to words and phrases that repeat. These are clues that you should combine some of your sentences to make your writing more clear and readable. Sentences can be combined in several different ways.

Using Modifiers to Combine

Many inexperienced writers find that they repeat words when describing something or someone. To correct these repetitions, remove the repeated words and use all the **modifiers** in one sentence. (Modifiers are words and phrases that describe.)

The school was old. **It was** out of date. **It** really needed remodeling.

The old school was out of date and needed remodeling

Using Phrases to Combine

Often, related sentences can be combined by using phrases to eliminate repeated words.

I worked hard all day. **I was working** at the store. **I was helping** in the produce section.

I worked hard at the store all day, helping in the produce section.

Using Clauses to Combine

Sometimes, writers combine sentences simply to make their writing sound smoother. When you notice that many of your sentences are short and choppy, change two or more related sentences into clauses and combine them. This will give variety to your writing. (Remember that clauses are word groups that contain a subject and a verb.)

You gave me a recipe book. I began cooking dinner every night.

After you gave me a recipe book, I began cooking dinner every night.

Getting Started

Read the following prompt and Samuel Nuñez's essay.

Prompt Your school board wants to limit the amount of homework assigned to students in grades one through eight. Would this help students to do better in school? Write a letter to your school board supporting your position.

Sample Essay

Homework Should Be Limited
by Samuel Nuñez

The school board members have been discussing an idea. They want to limit the amount of homework for all students in grades one through eight. This idea has upset some teachers and parents. **However, it has gained support among students and even some of the adults in the district. This support has been widespread.** Homework in the lower grades should be limited for many reasons, mainly because it does not contribute to student success. | 1
2
3
4
5
6
7

Homework in the lower grades places a burden. This burden is unfair. The burden falls on young children. However, children are not the only ones affected. Many times, parents must help their children with difficult assignments. By the time children finish their homework and eat dinner, their entire evening is over. **Children need time to relax. They need time to play. They will have enough time for work when they are adults.** | 8
9
10
11
12
13

Studies have shown that assigning lots of homework does not increase learning for young students. **They learn best in the classroom. They learn best with their teachers guiding them.** Sometimes parents are not sure what the teacher wants the students to do. **Instead of making children excited about learning, excessive homework becomes a source of frustration and confusion. It also adds to family stress.** | 14
15
16
17
18
19

In addition, homework sometimes contributes to student failure. When they are unable or unwilling to complete their homework, students receive low grades. Students develop low self-esteem. They develop poor attitudes toward school. Instead of helping them learn, homework often keeps students from learning. | 20
21
22
23

The school board should pass the ban on excessive homework. There is plenty of time for students to learn responsibility and time management once they are older. In the meantime, let most of their learning take place at school, and allow them to be children when they are at home. | 24
25
26
27

Looking It Over

1. Combine the bold sentences in lines 1–3 and 3–5 by using the methods you learned in this lesson. Write your two new sentences on the lines.

   _____

   _____

   _____

2. Look at the bold sentences in lines 8–9. Which word is repeated in these sentences?

   _____

3. Combine the bold sentences in lines 8–9 by using modifiers and phrases. Combine the bold sentences in lines 12–13 by using phrases and a semicolon to join two independent clauses. Write your two new sentences on the lines.

   _____

   _____

   _____

4. Combine the bold sentences in lines 15–16 by starting with the prepositional phrase "with their teachers guiding them." Write your new sentence on the line.

   _____

5. Combine the bold sentences in lines 17–19. Write your new sentence on the line.

   _____

6. Look at lines 20–23. Find one set of two sentences to combine, and write your combined sentence on the line.

   _____

7. How does combining sentences make Samuel's essay easier to read?

   _____

   _____

Writing Paragraphs

Paragraphs are groups of related ideas. When you organize the supporting details for the body of your essay, you should group related details together in paragraphs. Paragraphs help your readers see how you have organized your ideas. An essay without paragraphs is hard to read and understand.

Topic Sentence

Each body paragraph should begin with a topic sentence that tells your reader what the paragraph is about. This helps your reader follow your points more closely.

Supporting Details

You will usually have three to five sentences that support your topic in the middle of your paragraph. Your supporting details should include explanations, descriptions, and examples that support your topic sentence.

Concluding Sentence

Each paragraph should end with a concluding sentence that sums up the paragraph's message. The concluding sentence might also comment on the information in the supporting details. The concluding sentence signals that you are finished with this part of your essay. It lets your reader know that you are ready to move on to your next point.

Getting Started

Read the following prompt and the sample essay on the next page. Pay careful attention to the body paragraphs as you read. Then, answer the questions.

Prompt People grow up in all kinds of families, and all families are different. One thing that families have in common is the impact they have on the lives of individual family members. How has your family affected you as a person?

My Unique Family
by Mackenzie Haney

A | Everyone has a family, and most people have brothers and sisters. My family is a   1
bit different because I have no brothers or sisters. Even though it is small, I think   2
I have the best family in the world. Of course, they had a huge impact on the   3
person I have become.   4

B | One way my family has shaped my personality is through a deep interest in the   5
arts. My mother has always been active in community theater, and my father is   6
a musician who plays the violin and the guitar. Growing up surrounded by   7
music and drama has really made me aware of the arts in my life. I am involved   8
in both drama and band at school. I want to study music when I go to college.   9
I believe my parents' interest in the arts has had a direct influence on my own   10
interests.   11

C | My family has also encouraged my love of the outdoors. We all enjoy hiking   12
and camping, as well as gardening. For as long as I can remember, our best   13
times have been spent outdoors. We explore the woods around our home.   14
Then, we work together in our vegetable and flower gardens. I appreciate the   15
gift my parents have given me through their love of nature.   16

D | My family's most important contribution to my development has been the   17
constant feeling that they love me more than anything else in their lives. The   18
strength of their love and support has helped me try many things that I might   19
have been afraid to try alone. Whenever I feel sad, just knowing that I have two   20
people who care so much about me helps me feel better.   21

E | As you can see, I can directly trace many of my interests to my parents, and my   22
inner strength comes from knowing of their love for me. I feel lucky to call   23
them my family.   24

Looking It Over

Answer the questions below in the space provided.

1. What is the topic sentence of paragraph B? Does it let the reader know what
the paragraph is about?

   _____

   _____

2. List a detail in paragraph B that supports the claim that Mackenzie's parents
have encouraged her interest in music.

   _____

(continued on next page)

3. What is the topic of paragraph C?

_____

4. How does the last sentence of paragraph C "wrap up" the paragraph for the reader?

_____

_____

5. In paragraph D, Mackenzie states that the love of her parents helps her. In what two specific ways does their love help her?

_____

_____

6. Paragraph D does not have a concluding sentence. Write a concluding sentence that would be appropriate for this paragraph.

_____

Trying It Out

Write a paragraph that might appear in the body of an essay about being a teenager. Be sure to include supporting details to illustrate the point you are trying to make. Do not forget to write a concluding sentence at the end of your paragraph. Begin with the following topic sentence: **Being a teenager has definite advantages.**

_____

_____

_____

_____

_____

_____

_____

_____

_____

Making Transitions

Experienced writers know the importance of **transitions.** Transitions are words and phrases that show connections between sentences, phrases, and ideas.

Transitions can be used for many purposes. Some examples are listed below.

Transitions that add to ideas	further, besides, and, likewise, also, again, in addition, another, first, next, finally, last, not only
Transitions that show differences	but, yet, however, still, nevertheless, rather than, on the other hand, on the contrary, after all, at the same time, although
Transitions that show similarities	similarly, likewise, in a like manner, just as
Transitions that show results	therefore, accordingly, consequently, it follows that, as a result, so
Transitions that indicate time	meanwhile, immediately, soon, now, when, before, after, suddenly, during, finally, next
Transitions that indicate place	here, there, beyond, nearby, opposite to, next to, under, near
Transitions that summarize or highlight	in summary, in short, in other words, for example, for instance, in fact, indeed, in any event, as you can see, clearly

Getting Started

Read the following prompt. Then read the two body paragraphs from the sample essay on the next page. Pay careful attention to the transitions as you read. Then, answer the questions.

Prompt Many times, there is disagreement over whether students should be allowed to leave campus during lunch. What do you think would be the best solution for your school? Write a letter to your principal stating your position and telling why he or she should agree with your position.

Open Lunch, the Best Choice
by J.P. Osterling

One reason to allow students to leave campus during lunch is that leaving would   1
give students more choices. Rather than eating a bag lunch or whatever the   2
cafeteria is serving, students could choose from a variety of restaurants or even go   3
home to eat. Not only would students have more choice of foods, but they would   4
also have different locations to choose from. **On a nice spring day, students**   5
might decide to eat a picnic in a local park. As you can see, an open campus   6
during lunch would provide students with more freedom of choice.   7

In addition to the freedom it would give students, open lunch would also help   8
ease crowding in the cafeteria. As it is now, some students stand in line so long   9
that they have only a few minutes left to eat their food. **When students do**   10
manage to get their food, they must then face the challenge of finding a   11
place to sit. There are simply not enough places in the cafeteria; many students   12
end up sitting on the floor along the wall with their friends rather than   13
spending their time searching for a seat. Clearly, an open lunch policy would   14
help ease this problem, since fewer students would have to go to the cafeteria.   15

Looking It Over

1. Identify three transitions that J.P. uses in lines 1–7.

   _____

2. Look at the bold sentence in lines 5–6. What are two transitions you could use in this sentence?

   _____

3. Find two transitional words or phrases that J.P. uses in lines 8–15.

   _____

4. What transition could be used at the beginning of the bold sentence in lines 10–12? How could this transition help readers?

   _____

   _____

Trying It Out

1. The following paragraph does not have transitions to connect ideas. Find three places where a transition would be useful, and insert an appropriate transitional word or phrase.

My summer job was fun because it included many different tasks. I was an assistant at a local child-care center. Certain duties were my responsibility each day. I would help the cook serve breakfast to the children. I cleaned tables and emptied trash when the meal was finished. My main job was helping on the playground. I became quite good at doctoring little scrapes and bruises when the children fell. I enjoyed my summer job and hope to work there again next summer.

2. Write a paragraph explaining your household duties. Include at least three transitional words or phrases in your paragraph. Circle these transitions.

_____

_____

_____

_____

_____

_____

_____

_____

_____

Commonly Misspelled Words

When you are taking a writing test, it is important to spell words correctly. Like other errors, misspelled words can draw your reader's attention away from your message.

Study this list.

50 Frequently Misspelled Words

acquaint	experience	pleasant
across	false	privilege
athletic	February	realize
beautiful	film	recommend
benefit	finally	secretary
business	forty	separate
character	government	similar
clothes	grammar	since
committee	immediately	speech
decision	interesting	surprise
definite	knowledge	thorough
describe	library	together
description	minute	true
different	necessary	usually
disappear	ninety	Wednesday
disappoint	occasion	which
doctor	once	

Getting Started

Read the following prompt and the sample essay on the next page. Look for misspelled words. All misspelled words in the sample essay come from the list. Answer the questions when you have finished.

Prompt Your principal has agreed to allow a new club to form at your school. This club will be supported by a grant of money from the community. Write an editorial for your school newspaper suggesting a new club that you think would be worthy of the grant money.

Ecology Club
by Lisi Fakailoatonga

The whole school is talking about the community grant for a new club at our   1
school. I have heard many students suggesting diffrent clubs, and they all   2
sound great. The community, however, would benifit most from an ecology   3
club, wich would begin a school recycling program and organize park cleanups,   4
in addition to other projects.   5

An ecology club would help the school's students and staff to recycle. Every   6
day, baskets full of paper are thrown away in classrooms all over the school.   7
Most of this trash is recyclable, but nobody has organized an effort to recycle. 8
The club could place paper-recycling bins in each classroom immediatly as well   9
as take responsibility for emptying them and getting the paper to a recycling   10
center. The club would also take care of recycling aluminum soda cans from the 11
drink machines and similiar recyclable items. Any money that the program   12
might earn from recycling could then be placed in the club treasury to fund   13
other projects.   14

The club could also help make our city more beutiful. Club members could   15
organize special cleanup days, when students and community members would   16
work toghether to pick up trash, plant trees, and clear fallen brush in our city 17
parks. This experiense would help students realise the importance of taking care 18
of nature. It would also make our city parks more pleasent to visit.   19

A club that focuses on ecology would be the best choice for our school. It   20
would give students a chance to gain firsthand knowlege about our world and   21
our responsibility to care for it. I recomend that an ecology club be formed with 22
the community grant. It will be the best use of the city's money.   23

Looking It Over

Answer the questions below in the space provided.

1. Circle three misspelled words in lines 1–5. Write the correct words on the
   line.

   _____

2. Circle two misspelled words in lines 6–14. Write the correct words on the
   line.

   _____

3. Circle all the misspelled words in lines 15–23. Write the correct words on the
   line.

   _____

Trying It Out

Find and circle the misspelled words in the following sentences. Then, rewrite the sentences correctly on the lines provided. Sentences may have more than one misspelled word or none at all. If there are no misspelled words, write "correct."

1. I called the docter to schedule an appointment for either Tuesday or Wensday.

    _____

    _____

2. The day my grandfather turned ninety was a big family occasion.

    _____

    _____

3. The comittee's decision to ban certain styles of cloths was popular with parents.

    _____

    _____

4. Ever sense you asked me to meet you in the library, I have been counting the minites.

    _____

    _____

5. My friends gave me a suprise party wonce.

    _____

    _____

6. Last year I was in the atheletic program at school, but this year I want to get more involved in student goverment.

    _____

    _____

7. It dissapointed me to hear that I would not have the priviledge of participating in the rodeo in Febuary.

    _____

    _____

Commonly Misused Words

Words that sound alike but are spelled differently and have different meanings are called **homophones**. These words often cause problems for writers during writing tests. Learn these words, and remember to use them properly.

Common Homophones

- **ate**   Ian **ate** my apple.
  eight   I saw **eight** horses.

- **blue**   You have a **blue** car.
  blew   The wind **blew**.

- **buy**   I want to **buy** a bike.
  by   He sat **by** the door.

- **fair**   Was the test **fair**?
  fare   I paid your bus **fare**.

- **flower**   Smell this **flower**.
  flour   **Flour** is used in bread.

- **for**   This card is **for** you.
  four   Jaime sang **four** songs.

- **hear**   Can you **hear** me?
  here   Come **here**, please.

- **hour**   The class lasts an **hour**.
  our   Look at **our** new dog.

- **its**   The cat cleaned **its** fur.
  it's   **It's** really hot in here.

- **knot**   Can you tie a **knot**?
  not   I will **not** let you cheat.

- **meat**   Kim does not eat **meat**.
  meet   I want to **meet** her.

- **new**   Look at our **new** dog.
  knew   I **knew** the answer.

- **one**   We own **one** dog.
  won   Emilio **won** the race.

- **red**   She wore a **red** dress.
  read   I **read** the book myself.

- **right**   I got the **right** answer.
  write   Do you **write** poems?

- **road**   I live on a gravel **road**.
  rode   Khuyen **rode** the horse.

- **sea**   The **sea** tastes salty.
  see   Can you **see** the stage?

- **their**   They wiped **their** eyes.
  there   Put the pan over **there**.

- **threw**   Al **threw** me the ball.
  through   Go **through** the door.

- **to**   I sent it **to** you.
  too   You are **too** loud.
  too   She is loud, **too**.
  two   Grab **two** burgers.

- **weak**   I felt **weak**.
  week   It lasts for a **week**.

- **who's**   **Who's** the new kid?
  whose   **Whose** cap is that?

- **your**   Here is **your** cap.
  you're   **You're** my best friend

Getting Started

Circle the words that belong in each of the following sentences.

1. I was (weak, week) after playing for an (hour, our) in the heat.

2. Joanne (red, read) that book for class; it took her (for, four) days to finish it.

3. Mom only prepares (meat, meet) (to, two) times each (weak, week).

4. (Its, It's) (knot, not) (fair, fare) when you (buy, by) toys for Eduardo and (knot, not) (for, four) me.

5. Lin (new, knew) who (threw, through) the ball (threw, through) (hour, our) window.

Looking It Over

Make changes on the paragraphs to correct the misused homophones. The homophones appear in boldface. Not all boldface words are incorrect.

A. When our teacher told us about **hour** final exam, we all whined, "**Its** not **fair**!" She had included **for** essay questions, and we only had an **our** to finish them. Mrs. Jimenez told us we would **see** that the test would be fine. She was **write**. We all finished early, and **their** was time for a game afterward.

B. Last summer, my family visited the ocean for a **weak**. None of us had ever been **there** before; we even needed to use a map to find the **right rode**. The **see** was **not** as warm as I had imagined it would be. Perhaps that is because the wind **blue** the whole time we were **there**. I did **meet** some **knew** friends, and I hope we can go back before **to** long.

C. The quarterback **through** a long pass, hoping it would reach the receiver before the referee **blew** the whistle. Amazingly, it did, and our team **one** the game by only **four** points. "That was **to** close," I told my friend. "**Whose** having the victory party?" We all went to a pizza restaurant **four** dinner, and then we met back at the school for **hour** celebration of the victory.

Trying It Out

Write a paragraph on any topic, and use the following homophones correctly in the paragraph. Circle them as they appear in your paragraph. Use the space provided.

flower   see

one   their

red   knew

write   here

_____

_____

_____

_____

_____

_____

_____

_____

_____

_____

_____

_____

_____

_____

_____

_____

_____

Writing on Your Own

Read the following prompt. Prepare a written response to the prompt, keeping in mind what you have learned in this chapter.

Prompt Suppose that your school board is considering a plan to cancel all sports competitions. Do you feel sports competitions, such as football games and track meets, have a positive or a negative impact on your school? Write an essay telling your school board about your position on sports competitions, providing detailed support for your argument.

Remember the steps in writing a good essay.

Step 1. Write down the topic, audience, and purpose of an essay that responds to the prompt.

_____

_____

_____

Step 2. Use one of the prewriting methods you learned in Chapter 2, Lesson 2, to gather ideas for your essay.

Step 3. Look at your prewriting, and write a focus for your essay. Review Chapter 2, Lesson 3, if necessary.

_____

_____

Step 4. Use one of the organizational methods you learned in Chapter 2, Lesson 4, to order your essay's paragraphs.

(continued on next page)

Step 5 Write your essay. Keep in mind everything that you learned in this chapter.

_____

_____

_____

_____

_____

_____

_____

_____

_____

_____

_____

_____

_____

_____

_____

_____

_____

_____

_____

_____

_____

_____

_____

_____

_____

Evaluating Your Writing

As you learned in Chapter 2, Lesson 6, any essay you write for a test will be judged using a rubric. Use the rubric in Chapter 2, Lesson 6, to judge the essay you wrote on page 80. Then, answer the questions below to see how well you have applied the lessons of this chapter to your writing.

1. List the transitions you used in your essay. If you do not have **at least two** transitions per paragraph, go back and add more transitions.

    _____

    _____

    _____

    _____

2. Find three places in your essay where sentences could be combined to make the writing smoother. Write your new sentences below.

    _____

    _____

    _____

    _____

    _____

    _____

    _____

    _____

3. Read your paper out loud quietly to yourself, checking to make sure you have used commas appropriately. Include commas where they are needed, and remove any unnecessary commas. If you used a comma incorrectly, write the corrected sentence or sentences below.

    _____

    _____

    _____

(continued on next page)

4. As you read through your paper, circle any words that you think may be misspelled. If the words are not on the list in Lesson 7, look them up in a dictionary. Correct any words that are misspelled, and list the correct spellings below.

_____

_____

_____

_____

5. As you read over your essay, underline any homophones that you have used. Double-check these words to be sure you have used the correct word. Make any necessary changes. List the homophones (and changes, if any) below.

_____

_____

_____

_____

6. What is the strongest area of your essay? Why do you think so?

_____

_____

_____

_____

7. What is the weakest area of your essay? How could you improve it?

_____

_____

_____

_____

CHAPTER 4 REVIEW

Writing tests are a chance to show your writing skills, including your knowledge of the basic rules of the English language. Although content is important, do not forget to pay attention to paragraph structure, spelling, capitalization, punctuation, and word use.

Looking Back

Circle and correct the errors in the following sentences.

1. My Uncle and I road to the store. After I came home from school.

2. Jesse told me that "The cat hid under the bed."

3. It was hard to seperate the two puppies, finally we let them stay together?

4. Tasha if you turn East onto Orchard street you will find hour house.

5. Its to late, she told me as I tried to turn in yesterdays homework.

Combine and rewrite the following sentences on the lines provided.

6. Gabriel asked the teacher to help him. He asked quietly. He wanted help because he did not understand the assignment.

   _____

7. I left my umbrella at school. It is in the gym. I left it inside my locker.

   _____

8. Please call Andrea when you get home. Tell her about the project. The project is for science.

   _____

Trying It Out

Read the following prompt, and use your own paper to write an essay.

Prompt Many people feel that students who pass all required courses should be allowed to graduate from high school, even if they do not earn passing scores on state graduation exams. In a letter to your local newspaper, state your position on this issue, and support it with details and examples.

REVISING YOUR ESSAY

Introduction

When you revise your writing, you should try to see it through the eyes of your reader. Notice things your reader would notice. Does the body of your essay support the focus? Does each paragraph relate to the main idea of your essay? Are your sentences complete and correct? Once you look over your essay as a whole, you might decide certain sentences, or even certain sections, need to be rearranged or rewritten.

Looking for Mistakes

To begin revising, look for obvious mistakes and problems. Do you have sentence fragments, run-on sentences, or misspelled words? Note any paragraphs that are out of order or that need additional development.

Deciding What to Fix

When you take a writing test, you have to complete your essay in a certain amount of time. With limited time, you should first correct the major errors that would most interfere with the reader's ability to understand your essay. Then, go back to smaller errors.

Checklist for Revisions

Completing a checklist for revisions will help you make sure your writing is as good as possible. A revision checklist would include the following:

- Does your introduction clearly state your focus?

- Does your opening sentence grab the reader's attention?

- Does each paragraph support the focus?

- Is each sentence a complete thought?

- Are there any misspelled words?

Looking for Mistakes

Once you have written your essay, it is time to begin revising. Read through the entire piece and look for mistakes in grammar and organization. Make sure the essay has a clear focus and an effective introduction and conclusion.

Getting Started

Read the prompt and the essay. Notice the changes Lisa has made. When you finish, answer the questions.

Prompt Write an essay about an experience you had that has taught you something. Use specific examples.

Sample Essay

The Value of an After-School Job
by Lisa Chan

<u>Have you ever had to answer the phone, seat customers, and serve a dinner all</u>   1
<u>at once? I have</u>. I have been working at Sal's Seafood as a hostess for almost a   2
year. My job has taught me a great deal about working with others and   3
managing money. I think an after-school job can be a good experience for most   4
high school students.   5

When I received my first paycheck from Sal's, I was shocked. I thought ~~it would~~   6
~~be for a lot~~ <u>I would make</u> more money. I had worked over ten hours and ~~made~~   7
<u>earned</u> very little ~~money~~. <u>However, my</u> ~~My~~ job taught me how hard you have to   8
work to make money. It made me appreciate my mom and how hard she works   9
to support our family.   10

An after-school job also teaches you how to deal with people and how to work   11
with others. I learned how to calm a customer who was irritated because she   12
had to wait for a table. I also learned that most people depend on others to   13
help them do ~~there~~ <u>their</u> jobs. The servers at Sal's depended on me to seat   14
customers in their sections at an uneven pace so they didn't have to too many   15
tables to serve. ~~So an after-school job teaches you a lot about other people~~.   16
<u>I also learned that I depended on others in the restaurant to pitch in and help</u>   17
<u>me when I was busy.</u>   18

<u>In conclusion,</u> I think most high school ~~student's~~ students would benefit from   19
working an after-school job. They would learn a ~~grate~~ <u>great</u> deal about   20
managing money and working with others. An after-school job would also help   21
prepare them for life after high school.   22

Looking It Over

1. Read the entire essay and note Lisa's revisions. What is the essay's focus? Write the focus in your own words.

   _____

   _____

2. Lisa added a sentence at the beginning of the essay. Why did she do this?

   _____

   _____

3. Why did Lisa cut out the last sentence in line 16? Why did she add a new sentence in this paragraph?

   _____

   _____

Trying It Out

Read the following prompt and essay. On your own paper, revise the essay to fix any mistakes.

> **Prompt** We admire people for many different reasons. They may be very brave, kind, or hardworking. Choose the person you admire most and discuss what makes this person special.

> **Sample Essay**
>
> ### My Brother Ryan
> ### by Marc Martino
>
> Although my brother Ryan can't see with his eyes the way most people do, he   1
> sees much better than anyone else I know. Ryan likes just about everybody he   2
> meets and he brings out the best in people with his attitude. Ryan can tell   3
> when the sun is shining. Because he can feel its warmth. He knows when its   4
> about to rain because he can smell the dampness in the air. Ryan sees people   5
> best of all. Although Ryan can't tell for sure how people look, he gets to no   6
> them by what they say and do.   7
>
> It isn't easy being blind. Ryan is a very strong person. Ryan has to use a cane   8
> too help him find his way around. However, Ryan never complains. He is always   9
> smiling and tries to make other people feel good. Ryan is always there for me.   10
> Ryan sets a great example to follow.   11

Deciding What to Fix

When you take a writing test, you may have only a few minutes to revise your essay. You have to decide what errors to fix in the time you have available. For example, you do not want to spend all of your time revising one sentence if your essay has major mistakes. Before you revise your essay, make sure it has a focus. Check to make sure each of your paragraphs supports your focus. Next, make sure each paragraph has enough sentences to make your point. Then, fix any noticeable errors. Look for sentence fragments and verbs that do not agree with subjects. Are there any misspelled or missing words?

Getting Started

Read the following prompt and essay. Take note of Genelle's revisions.

Prompt Think of a problem that affects the people who live in your community. Explain the problem, and suggest a solution.

Sample Essay

A Place for In-Line Skaters
by Genelle Davidowitz

Some people in my town recently attended a town council meeting and   1
complained about teenagers who in-line skate on sidewalks and streets. They   2
told council members that the skating disturbings the peace, ~~makes too much~~ 3
~~noise,~~ and damages property. They want a law passed. The law would make it   4
illegal to skate on the streets or sidewalks in our town.   5

Passing such a law is unfair. In-line skating is fun and is good physical exercise. 6
Teenagers skating are not doing anything wrong or harming anyone. We teens   7
need a place to skate. If the citizens don't want us near their property, the town 8
should build a special in-line skating park. A park would give us a place to skate. 9
It would limit the ~~amount~~number of in-line skaters on our town's streets.   10

Looking It Over

On a separate sheet of paper, answer the following questions.

1. Look over Genelle's essay. What types of changes did she make?

2. Why did she delete the phrase "makes too much noise" in lines 3–4?

3. If Genelle had more time, what additional changes could she have made? Circle two sentences that should be revised.

Trying It Out

Read the following prompt and sample essay. Fix only the obvious mistakes, and make only **five** revisions to the essay. Choose the most noticeable and important errors. Mark your changes on the essay.

Prompt Teachers can be important people in our lives. Choose a favorite teacher and explain what makes this teacher special.

Sample Essay

Mr. Sanchez
by Emile Rodriguez

I had Mr. Sanchez for history, a subject that is usually very boring to me. Mr.   1

Sanchez often dressed up like famous historical characters. He always looked   2

funny. He made everyone laugh. Once he dressed up as George Washington,   3

another time he dressed up as Abraham Lincoln. Mr. Sanchez liked to crack   4

jokes to. We had a good time in his class.   5

Sometimes he would make us act out what we were studying. Once we builded   6

a model of an Egyptian pyramid out of cardboard boxes. Another time we   7

pretended to live in an ancient Sumerian city. Even though we sometimes   8

laughed and felt really silly when we were acting things out, we really learned   9

about what we were studying. I still remember many of the things that Mr.   10

Sanchez taught me.   11

Checklist for Revisions

In order to write the best essay possible, use a checklist for revisions. A checklist for revisions should begin with the most important items. When you are taking a writing test, you may not have time to check each item on the checklist. However, if the most important items are listed first, you might have time to check those.

Getting Started

Consider the following checklist:

1. Does your essay respond to the writing prompt?
2. Does your introduction clearly state your focus?
3. Does the body of your essay support your focus?
4. Does your essay have a conclusion?
5. Does each paragraph contain a topic sentence?
6. Does each paragraph discuss only one idea?
7. Are there smooth transitions between paragraphs?
8. Does your essay have a title?
9. Does your opening sentence grab the reader's attention?
10. Have you combined short, awkward sentences?
11. Have you fixed all sentence fragments and run-on sentences?
12. Have you crossed out any unnecessary words?
13. Do your verbs agree with your subjects?
14. Does each pronoun agree with its antecedent?
15. Have you used correct punctuation and spelling?

Looking It Over

1. Look over the checklist one more time. What is the meaning of the question "Do your verbs agree with your subjects?" Write a sentence in which the verb agrees with its subject.

   _____

   _____

   _____

2. Add something to the checklist for revisions that would help you when you are revising your own writing.

   _____

   _____

CHAPTER 5 REVIEW

In this chapter, you have learned about the final steps required to do well on a writing test. When you are taking a writing test, you will not have much time to fix mistakes. You will have to be an efficient reviser. You have learned the following skills for revising your essay effectively:

● look for mistakes

● choose which mistakes to fix

● use a checklist to help you revise

Now that you have learned how to revise your answers on writing tests, you are truly prepared to do well on any writing exam.

Trying It Out

Read the sample prompt and essay. Revise the essay using the checklist for revisions.

Prompt To improve students' grades and test scores, your school is considering extending the school year until the end of July. Explain whether you think this is a good idea and why you feel this way.

Sample Essay

Shorter Is Better
by Walter Davidson

Extended the school year until the end of July is not a good idea and will not	1
improve students' grades or test scores. For starters, we student's are tired by	2
the middle of June. The end of our school year now. We can't possible learn any	3
more. We really time away from school to relax. We need to spend time with	4
our friends and families. Time off during the summer helps us learn better in the	5
fall. When we return to school. Its also more harder to learn when its warm	6
outside, we becomes distracted and want to do other things, like spending time	7
at the beach or going hiking and camping outdoors. Warm weather is a great	8
time for outdoor activities.	9
Some students work during the summer. They depends on this income to buy	10
clothes and other things that you need during the school year. If the school	11
year went into July, these students would not be able to earn the money they	12
need. I think that extending the school year is a bad idea and will hurt students	13
in the long run.	14

OTHER KINDS OF WRITING FOR TESTS

Introduction

Most writing tests will ask you to write an essay such as the four you saw earlier. However, some writing tests ask you to write a letter or a report. The basic elements of focus, support, and organization will help you write effective letters and reports. The differences will be in the form of the writing and your audience.

Other kinds of writing include the following:

- **Friendly letter:** The prompt may ask you to write to a friend, relative, or acquaintance.

- **Business letter:** The prompt may ask you to write to a businessperson, a government official, or a newspaper or magazine editor.

- **Report:** The prompt may ask you to write a short report based on a list of facts. Since the report is informational, it will be like an expository essay.

Keep in mind that any kind of letter you write is directed toward an audience. A letter to someone you know will be less formal, though it should never be sloppy. You should choose more formal language in a business letter or report. A letter to the editor of a newspaper is written to be published in the newspaper. In that case, your audience is the newspaper's readers, not the editor.

On any writing test, remember that your writing should show how well you can write. Although a prompt may call for a letter to a friend or relative, your written response will be scored the same way an essay would be scored. Even a letter should be focused and well organized, with supporting statements.

Letters and Reports

The parts of a **friendly letter** are

- date
- salutation, or greeting
- body
- closing
- signature

A **business letter** has all of these parts, and adds

- heading
- inside address
- typed name and title under the signature

Getting Started

Read the following prompt and letter. Look for elements of the persuasive essay in the body. Think about how the letter could be changed to a business letter. Then, answer the questions.

Prompt Your high school class is planning to clean up the local lake as a community-service project. You would like to have friends volunteer for the day. Write a letter to a friend promoting the event and asking for help.

Sample Letter

	March 1, 2002 1

Dear Josephine,   2

Have you been to Lake Warton recently? It is a mess. The senior class of   3
Wartonville High School, with the help of friends and employers in town, plans   4
to clean up Lake Warton as a part of our community service on May 23. As the   5
senior class president, I am asking the junior class to help out.   6

All of your class will have the chance to enjoy the sun, be involved in the   7
community, and get some exercise. Your classmates will also see firsthand how   8
to do their own community-service project.   9

I hope you can all help us. I must hear from you by April 12. For more details   10
please contact our principal Mr. Nguyen or me at 555–2134.   11

Always,   12

Kitren Oforstendahl   13

Looking It Over

1. Look at Kitren's letter. How would you change it to make it a business letter? What three parts would you add? What punctuation would you change?

   _____

   _____

   _____

2. If Kitren were sending her letter to a business, what changes would she make?

   _____

   _____

Trying It Out

Read the two prompts below and respond to one of them. Use your own paper.

Letter Prompt Your town leaders are thinking about holding outdoor concerts in the park this summer. Some people look forward to the opportunity to enjoy music with their neighbors. Others fear that the concerts will be noisy and annoying. Write a letter to the editor of a local newspaper, stating your views on this topic. Be sure to support your opinions with good reasons.

Report Prompt Your teacher has told you that you can write a report for extra credit. The topic is famous buildings in Washington, D.C. Below are the notes you have taken. Write a report (an expository essay) based on the notes below.

Notes:

● Washington, D.C.—our nation's capital

● the Capitol Building—started in 1793; completed in 1863

● Washington Monument—honors George Washington;begun building in 1848; finished in 1884

● Congress meets in Capitol Building

● White House—designed by James Hoban

● 555 feet, 5 inches—height of Washington Monument

● White House—begun building in 1792; completed in 1800

● over 300 memorials and statues in Washington, D.C.

● British burned White House in War of 1812; rebuilt by 1817

GLOSSARY

body: the middle paragraphs of an essay. A typical essay includes an introductory paragraph, several body paragraphs, and a concluding paragraph. Pages 8, **14–15**.

brainstorming: a prewriting method that involves writing down any idea that comes to mind, usually in the form of a list. Page **24**.

chronological order: a method of organizing an essay according to the timing of events mentioned in the essay. Page **30**.

conclusion: an essay's last paragraph. The conclusion restates the essay's focus and main points while bringing the essay to a close. A typical essay includes an introduction, a body, and a conclusion. Pages 8, **14–15**.

descriptive essay: an essay that describes. Its primary purpose is to describe things, places, or people. Pages 38, 40, **50–52**.

expository essay: an essay that explains. Its primary purpose is to present information. Pages 38, 39, **41–43**.

focus: the main idea of an essay, also called the central idea or the thesis. Pages **8**, 10, 21, 27.

freewriting: a prewriting method that involves writing down any idea that comes to mind, usually in the form of phrases and sentences. Page **24**.

introduction: an essay's first paragraph, which introduces the topic and states the essay's focus. A typical essay includes an introduction, a body, and a conclusion. Pages 8, **14–15**.

letter to the editor: a persuasive letter written to the editor of a newspaper or magazine but intended to be read by the general public. Pages **91**, 93.

logical order: a method of organizing an essay to connect related ideas in a way that makes sense. For instance, an essay about pets might discuss cats in one section, dogs in a second section, and hamsters in a third section. Page **30**.

GLOSSARY

narrative essay: an essay that tells a story. Pages 38, 40, **47–49**.

order of importance: a method of organizing an essay according to the importance of the paragraph topics. Ideas in an essay are often arranged from least important to most important. Page **30**.

persuasive essay: an essay that attempts to persuade. The primary purpose of a persuasive essay is to persuade the reader to believe something or to take some action. Pages 38, 39, **44–46**.

prompt: an essay assignment, usually in the form of a short paragraph outlining an essay topic, the audience for which the essay will be written, and the purpose of the essay. Some prompts include a picture to inspire the writer. Pages 21, **22–23**.

revision: the process of improving an essay after the first draft is written. Pages 35–36, 81–82, **85–90**.

rubric: a checklist of the key elements of a good essay, used as a tool for evaluating writing. Pages **18**–19, 35–36.

salutation: the greeting in a formal or informal letter. It usually takes the form: "Dear_____" and is followed by a comma or colon. Page **92**.

spatial order: a method of organizing an essay according to the physical arrangement of items discussed in the essay. For instance, a description of a mall might start at one end of the mall and move to the other. Page **30**.

supporting details: ideas within a paragraph that support the topic sentence of the paragraph. There are usually several supporting details in each body paragraph of an essay. Page **67**.

topic sentence: the sentence, often at the beginning of a paragraph, that states the main idea of the paragraph. In the body paragraphs of an essay, the topic sentences will express the point the paragraph makes to support the focus. Page **67**.

Test-Taking Tips

In this book, you have learned many useful skills to help you succeed on writing tests. Here are a few additional test-taking hints.

- Be sure that you are well-rested and physically ready for the test. Get a good night's sleep. Be sure to eat a good breakfast. Avoid drinking anything with caffeine before the test. Caffeine can make you nervous and interfere with your ability to think. Visit the bathroom before the test begins.

- Wear comfortable clothes. Bring a sweater in case the room is cold.

- Bring pens, pencils, erasers, and anything else you will need.

- Before the test, take a moment to relax. Take a deep breath, and remind yourself that you are prepared. Tell yourself that you have been taught well and that you will do well on the test. If you feel tense, you can squeeze the desk with your hands to release tension. Breathing deeply and slowly will also help you relax.

- When the test is handed out, quickly scan the prompts to see how many essays you will need to write. Be sure to check the instructions so that you know whether you will need to respond to all of the prompts or just some of them.

- Read each prompt twice before writing.

- Take note of how much time you have to finish the test. Budget your time so that you have time to prewrite. Leave time for revising, but schedule most of your time for writing.

- Do not start writing until you have a plan for your essay. Complete your essay before you start revising. On most tests, it is more important to have a complete essay than a perfect one.